Gift from of Friends of Library

Dear Mom, I've Always Wanted You to Know . . .

A Perigee Book

Dear Mom, I've Always Wanted You to Know

Daughters Share Letters from the Heart

Lisa R. Delman

THE BERKLEY PUBLISHING GROUP
Published by the Penguin Group
Penguin Group (USA) Inc.
375 Hudson Street, New York, New York 10014, USA
Penguin Group (Canada), 10 Alcorn Avenue, Toronto, Ontario M4V 3B2, Canada
(a division of Pearson Penguin Canada Inc.)
Penguin Books Ltd., 80 Strand, London WC2R 0RL, England
Penguin Group Ireland, 25 St. Stephen's Green, Dublin 2, Ireland (a division of Penguin Books Ltd.)
Penguin Group (Australia), 250 Camberwell Road, Camberwell, Victoria 3124, Australia
(a division of Pearson Australia Group Pty. Ltd.)
Penguin Books India Pvt. Ltd., 11 Community Centre, Panchsheel Park, New Delhi - 110 017, India
Penguin Group (NZ), cnr Airborne and Rosedale Roads, Albany, Auckland 1310, New Zealand
(a division of Pearson New Zealand Ltd.)
Penguin Books (South Africa) (Pty.) Ltd., 24 Sturdee Avenue, Rosebank, Johannesburg 2196, South Africa

Penguin Books Ltd., Registered Offices: 80 Strand, London WC2R 0RL, England

This book is an original publication of The Berkley Publishing Group.

Copyright © 2005 by Lisa Delman.
Cover design by Ben Gibson.
Text design by Tiffany Estreicher.

First Perigee hardcover edition: April 2005

Library of Congress Cataloging-in-Publication Data

Delman, Lisa R. (Lisa Rachel)
    Dear Mom, I've always wanted you to know— : daughters share letters from the heart / by
Lisa R. Delman.—1st Perigee hardcover ed.
       p. cm.
    Includes bibliographical references.
    ISBN 0-399-53079-7
    1. Mothers and daughters. 2. Daughters—Correspondence. 3. Daughters—Psychology.
I. Title.

HQ755.86.D45 2005
306.874'3—dc22   2004053360

PRINTED IN THE UNITED STATES OF AMERICA

10 9 8 7 6 5 4 3 2 1

Most Perigee Books are available at special quantity discounts
for bulk purchases for sales promotions, premiums, fund-raising
or educational use. Special books, or book excerpts, can also be
created to fit specific needs.

For details, write: Special Markets, The Berkley Publishing
Group, 375 Hudson Street, New York, New York 10014.

Dear Mom,
Thank you for reminding me that life is precious.
Truly from my heart, I dedicate this book to you, Mother.

Contents

Acknowledgments   xi

Foreword   xiii

Introduction—
Awakening the "Mother" Within   1

The Gift of Gratitude   10

Embracing Sweet Sorrow   38

Leaving Shame Behind   61

Freedom from Anger   86

Goodbye to Guilt   113

From Abandonment to Wholeness   138

The Choice to Forgive   165

The Courage to Grieve   191

Realizing Love   211

The Need for Closure: 240

A Loving Word from Lisa
An Invitation to You   244

Ten Ways to Open Your Heart to Your Mother   246

About the Author   251

There are no mistakes, no coincidences.
All events are blessings given to us to learn from.

Elisabeth Kubler-Ross

Acknowledgments

The birth of this book and the Letters from the Heart Project™ would have not been possible without the infinite wisdom, inspiration, and love from my family, friends, and teachers. I carry their knowledge and beauty within my heart every moment.

Thanks to my parents, sister, and brother for their unconditional love throughout my life.

Infinite gratitude goes to the courageous women letter writers around the world. You have opened my heart in more ways than you can imagine.

I am so blessed to have received the insightful teachings of Chaim Daskal, the sage for many around the world.

To my great partners and angels in my life that have, in their special ways, contributed to the birth of the Letters from the Heart Project™: Dianne Collins, the creator of QuantumThink®, Robert Shemin, Alisa Battaglia, Susan Abel, David Potter, Cynthia Greenawalt, Alan Collins, cofounder of QuantumThink® Grace Cruz, Buffy Gandon, Debbie Daley, Debbie Milam, Liz Sterling, Richelle Doliner, Irene Mann, Elena Bou, Luba Bozanich, Toby Bass, Lynn Page, and Denise Soler. Especially to Kathleen Potter, for her special contribution toward the development of this book.

I offer many thanks for those who have nurtured this book from inception to completion. First among them is my agent, Lori Perkins, who wholeheartedly believed in the vision, before it was scribbled on paper. To Sheila Curry Oakes, who encouraged me to refine my work, Kathryn McHugh for taking the ball and running with it, Adrienne Schultz, my editor, for guiding me gently through the manuscript, to Kim Koren, John Duff, Terri Hennessey, and all the other talented people at Perigee who shaped this book into what it is. To my consulting editor, Barbara McNichol, for her endless hours of dedication, support, and expertise in editing. To Sam Horn for her laser coaching in getting to the heart of the matter quickly. To Heidi Richards for her fabulous flowers. To Dave Bell, Raleigh Pinskey, Sheryl Roush, Jill Dahne, Dr. Maura Cohen, and the many others for their insight, enthusiasm, and belief in me. To Ron Tarantino for challenging and motivating me to be the best I can be.

I am especially grateful to my wonderful husband and soulful partner, John, for giving me the support and freedom to follow my life's mission. He is the wise warrior I saw in my dreams. Because of his love and life experiences, I have the compassion needed to forge forward into uncharted territory.

foreword

For over a decade, I have done my best to impart an important message to the thousands of people whom I coach and train each year: The relationships, circumstances, and parts of ourselves that we resist the most are the ones that have the most to teach us. Our relationship with our mothers is probably the best example of this essential truth. Whether we adore them, can't stand to be in the same room with them, or have spent very little time with them at all, our motheres have shaped our personalities, influenced our core beliefs, and have had a dramatic effect on the people we have become.

So the question arises: If our mothers have so much to teach us, why do many of us put up walls that prevent us from receiving their wisdom? I believe we resist exploring the hidden layers of our relationships with our mothers becacuse at some level we are terrified of what we might find. Maybe we're afraid that we won't live up to their expectations. Maybe we fear that our attempts to reach out will be met with indifference or rejection. And perhaps most of all, maybe we're afraid to discover that we are just like our mothers. Whatever our fears, our projections, or our reasons, the fact remains that many of us opt to leave this vital relationship unexplored. Instead, we put our energy into developing coping mechanisms to manage the relationship so they appear to be just "fine." But these are just a defense that keeps us from experiencing the true benefits and intimacy of mother love. Often, it's not until we become intimately involved with another, or become parents ourselves, that we are willing to explore our most primary relationship of all. Watching as our childhood patterns repeat themselves over and over again is sometimes all the incentive we need to try to understand in earnest the events, relationships, and experiences that have made us who we are.

Dear Mom, I've Always Wanted You to Know is a steady guide that can support you through the complex and often scary terrain of making peace with your mother. The process of baring your soul, unraveling your suppressed emotions, and speaking from your heart will liberate you and bring light to all areas of your life. I promise you that by exploring your relationship with your mother and finding the willingness to forgive her flaws and transgressions, you will receive the greatest gift of all: emotional freedom.

by Debbie Ford

Dear Mom, I've Always Wanted You to Know . . .

Awakening the "Mother" Within

I was flooded with so many emotions as my mother lay in a coma from a massive heart attack. Tears welled up and washed away the trivial worries of the past. I was overwhelmed by the fear, sadness, and pain that throbbed deep within my heart.

Shocked by the thought of losing my mother, I grappled with these questions: What if I were never again able to hear my mother's voice on the telephone? What if I had no time left to tell my mother how I felt? How would I cope without her? At that crucial moment, I was reminded of the impermanence of life and how the simplest things were my greatest treasures.

During this family crisis, I chose to tuck away my emotions so I had strength to give to my mother, father, and sister. I couldn't let myself fall apart at a time when my mother needed me most. If I succumbed to the doctor's pronounce-ment that she only had a 20 percent chance to live, I would have been devastated. So I stayed highly focused on my de-cision to connect with her heart to heart, permeating her soul with my own positive energy.

In doing so, my heart opened to a place of surrender and vulnerability. I prayed more than I'd ever prayed in my life that we could share many more years together.

As if my mother were speaking to me, I heard a voice say, "There you go again, telling me what to do. It's my choice whether I live or die." Out of quiet desperation, I replied, "You're right, Mom. It is your choice." The next day, she came out of the coma.

Miraculously, my mother did fully recover. Yet I had postponed feeling my own pain until she was well. I was stuck in grief at the thought of losing her. I felt the appre-hension of inevitable loss and abandonment, worried how my father would cope, and feared experiencing womanhood without my mother. Above all, I was haunted by the fear of never being able to speak about the newfound appreciation I had for her.

I also knew that letting go of my grief would be crucial for my growth as a woman, and I was ready to begin my journey of renewal. This led me to working with a wise coach and teacher, Chaim Daskal, who guided me through a series of exercises to release the feelings trapped deep in my core. All the processes had a profound effect on me, yet one exercise changed my life forever. Chaim inspired me to write a soulful letter to my mother, articulating in writing all the things I wanted to communicate to her—before it was too late.

Letter Writing—The Start of a Journey

"How will writing letters make my mother and me better together?" I asked Chaim. He told me, "Concentrate first on releasing your words. Then, when you read them, this will cause a healing. Keep on writing until you are finished."

Although I had participated in many courses to delve deeper within myself, I'd never explored letter writing as an outlet for self-expression. I felt great relief from articulating my emotions on paper privately. Certainly, a part of me felt sorrowful for not recognizing the importance of my female roots earlier.

Heeding Chaim's advice, I furiously translated my deepest thoughts in a series of eleven letters. Traveling for the first time to this place in my heart, I viewed my mother—and our relationship—from a new perspective. By writing *to* my mother instead of *about* her, I was able to see reflections of myself and become accountable for my part of our relationship. I understood that my feelings of resentment were about *me* and began to empathize with her as a woman more than a mother. And as I embraced her challenges and triumphs in a compassionate way, I was graciously able to accept my own humanity.

A Grander Vision

I had not planned to do anything more with my letters. Yet as I told others about the catharsis I had experienced, a grander vision was waiting in the wings. Their empathic responses painfully reminded me that, unfortunately, most women have unfinished business, unspoken emotions, and unfulfilled relationships with their mothers.

Eager to hold a divine space in which women could connect deeply with their hearts, I created the Letters from the Heart Project™. I set up a letter-writing contest through the Web site (www.LettersFromTheHeartProject.com) where I asked participants to write letters to their mothers that expressed their deepest emotions and offered insight into their own journeys. These guidelines assured them a safe place to be heard and a sacred way to reveal their innermost feelings. In my role of facilitator, I wanted to inspire them to look within for their own answers.

I received more than a thousand poignant entries from women around the world. Every compelling and thought-provoking letter conveyed the feelings, struggles, and victories of everyday living, the complexities of the daughter-mother relationship, and the rawness of humanity that intricately connects us. Many women experienced a catharsis similar to mine. As Sarah Nguyen wrote, "The experience of writing to my mother was amazing. Not only was I able to pour my heart out, but I was also able to become free of a burden I didn't even know I was carrying."

At first, I thought this Project would focus on the theme of forgiveness. But as I gained insight into these writers' lives, I realized, along with forgiveness, their stories depicted all other central emotions of our hearts: love, sorrow, grief, abandonment, anger, resentment, guilt, shame, and gratitude.

The letters came from a diverse group of women from India, Israel, Norway, the Philippines, the Dominican Republic, England, Ireland, Australia, New Zealand, Africa, Russia, Canada, Puerto Rico, and many parts of the United States. Ranging in age from fourteen to seventy-five, they are single mothers, motherless daughters, handicapped women, retired women, homeless teenagers, heterosexual women, homosexual women, foster mothers, and grandmothers. They are poets, scholars, authors, psychologists, social workers, doctors, students, accountants, secretaries, lawyers, business owners, homemakers, and teachers. These women have revealed their most intimate secrets in letters to their mothers. Some have chosen anonymity to protect their privacy. All deserve sensitivity, respect, and compassion for their extraordinary courage.

Although I hold each letter as valuable, I could choose only a cross section to include in this book. In no way does this imply that the other letters lacked significance. Each letter stands powerfully as a symbol of the writers liberation from disappointments and unfulfilled expectations. Helen Chen said, "My mom passed away suddenly. There were so many things that I wanted to tell her but didn't. After I heard about the Letters from the Heart Project™, twice, I tried to write the letter but ended up crying the whole night without putting down a single word. Finally, I took a day off from work and wrote my letter. After I finished it, for a long time, I lay on the floor and could not think or move—as if my soul had left me. When I finally got up from the floor, I had this reborn feeling and somehow I knew that my mother had received and responded to my letter. I was able to let go of the past, somehow assured that she would never leave me, no matter what."

Begin Now

You may tell yourself it's not a priority to write a letter. You don't know where to begin, you're not good at this introspective stuff, or you're simply frightened. I validate your concerns that it's scary to delve into your emotions. It's because we welcome positive feelings with enthusiasm and vigor. Yet it is human nature to sidestep unpleasant ones, just as we sidestep household chores. But just as with chores, the more we avoid them, the more they fester inside and eventually reveal themselves. As we learn to embrace our shadows as part of our light, we can move in and out of our emotions more gracefully. Like an exquisite tapestry, we can see how the threads of our negative and positive emotions play a vital role in awakening the best part of ourselves. Learning to articulate our innermost feelings is an ongoing process that takes patience, courage, and tenderness.

Using letter writing to explore our feelings toward "mother" initiates this heartfelt journey—one that leads to connection, gratitude, and emotional closure in the most primal relationship we have. Letter writing is an essential tool that can be used in every religion, philosophy, therapy, support group, or challenge that people experience. All it requires is a willingness to begin and to trust yourself.

The value of writing is affirmed by Thomas Moore, author of *Care of the Soul,* who described it as the reflection of our soul, the essence of expression. Thich Nhat Hanh, Buddhist monk, peace activist, and author of *Anger* affirmed its value by writing, "Take one, two, or even three weeks to finish your letter, because it is a very important letter. The letter is crucial to your happiness."

The letter-writing process is not about dumping ill will on your mother. It's about resolving past hurts, seeing your challenges in a new light, and experiencing shifts within yourself and your relationship with her. Above all, it is about releasing emotion and freeing *yourself.* (If at any point in this letter-writing journey you need assistance from a health professional, please seek it.)

Permission to Explore

Reading these letters will give you permission to explore your innermost feelings without judgment from others. You may be compelled to "visit" one chapter more than another. Open your heart and know that your emotional journey requires no particular order. Use the experiences of these writers to guide you to answer your own questions in your own time. I encourage you to write any insights you may have on the blank pages of a journal.

Because of my mother's miraculous recovery and our healing process together, the Letters from the Heart Project™ was born to help other women find their voices. I hope these letters will help you realize, as I did, that letting go of the past is essential to having a joyous life.

This book stands as an inquiry into the soul, an invitation for you, dear reader, to become open to rich places within. I hope you will be inspired to write a letter to your own mother, whether she is alive or not. However you choose to communicate, I challenge you to express what needs to be said now—for now is truly all you have.

Truly, Lisa Rachel Delman

The Gift of Gratitude

When one looks for things to appreciate in a mother, no matter how small and how remote, the heart opens and finds more and more good things to remember. The blessings bridge the gap we once thought was too huge to cross.

P. ARGO, *India*

Our journeys begin as we bask in our mothers' protective wombs, clinging to their every breath to nourish our souls. They embrace us for the first time in their loving arms, providing us protection and unconditional acceptance. We can imagine their first tears, hear their first laughs, and feel their soft kisses. Our mothers treasure this joyous occasion with all their hearts.

As we honor the miraculous process of birth, we can appreciate our mothers, at the very least, for giving us our lives. If we can find one thing to be grateful for, we can at least begin appreciating our mothers in a newfound way.

As a little girl, I did not think about how much I appreciated my mother. I always loved her. Not until my mother almost lost her life did I realize how much I took her for granted. Certainly, a part of me felt sorrowful for not recognizing the importance of my female roots earlier. Nevertheless, I was eternally grateful for recognizing this moment of appreciation.

Beckie Miller, in writing her letter for the project, had a similar experience. "I also remembered my mom of long ago . . . before life's painful events sapped her of her joy. It allowed me to come to a greater understanding for emotional frailty." As we contemplate the lives of these women through the letters that follow, we become profoundly aware that resentment and gratefulness can't coexist. Our level of gratefulness toward our mothers solely depends on what we hold onto and what we are willing to let go of. Many of us still blame our mothers for our not fitting in the role we imagined for ourselves. Others of us may love our mothers, yet there is a part of us that feels frustrated by a perceived lack of support or understanding. Some of us say our lives are better without them. Yet if we always focus on our negativity toward our mothers, we will continue to be disconnected from our roots.

Rabbi Freeman's newsletter *Daily Dose of Wisdom* says, "The beginning of all paths and the foundation of all ascents is to open yourself to receive." If we empty our vessels of resentment, we once again are able to receive the gifts of our mothers as witnessed in this book. Allowing ourselves our first step in awakening ourselves to new possibilities, many of us eagerly search for answers to our unanswered questions.

We can reach a level of appreciation through letting go of our anguish. After all, who we are—as girls, daughters, and women—is greatly shaped by our relationships with our mothers. Our level of gratefulness depends on the foundation we had with our mothers; the awakening of our selves depends on it, too, and so does our renewal of life.

We may be asking, "What do I have to be grateful for?" Let's begin with appreciating our mothers.

How Much You Mean to Me

*My greatest fear is I will never tell you how much you
mean to me. This letter is my way of ending the fear.*
SHELLEY ANN WAKE, *Australia*

Dearest Mom,
I am scared of a lot of things. Of being at home alone on a
dark night, of putting on a shoe and finding a spider at the
bottom of it, of waking up old and finding my life has passed
me by. But there is only one fear that really hurts right to the
bottom of my heart. That fear is that I will never be able to
tell you how much you mean to me.

I don't know when it happened, but sometime so long
ago, I grew up and forgot to talk honestly. I can't remember
telling you that I love you even once. That saddens me in so
many ways—mostly just to think that you are the most important person in my life and maybe you don't know it. Or
that you don't realize how much I appreciate every little
thing you have ever done for me.

Throughout my whole life, you put me first. From buying me the best presents every Christmas and birthday to making me dinner every night to always telling me I could be whatever I wanted to be. I believed you when you said it, and I still do. I owe it to you for the strength that I have.

When I was seventeen, I told you I was going to marry someone—not even because I loved him, but because I felt I had to. He was going away to start a career and said he wouldn't go without me. I didn't want to stop him from starting his career, so I said yes.

You told me there was nothing you would do to stop me, but you thought I would regret it forever. You were right; I would have. But somehow I found the strength to break his heart and tell him no. I can see now how wrong it would have been; I can see how clear that was to you. But even though you could see that, you just told me calmly to think about it carefully. You had faith enough in me to believe that I would make the right decision. It made all the difference in the world.

There are a thousand other times when you could see I was wrong, but you let me make up my own mind. You let me make mistakes because you knew I needed to learn from them. Now I am able to make my own decisions. This is just one of the ways you have made me who I am today—a strong, independent woman.

These are things I have never told you. Sometimes I wonder if you know how much I appreciated everything. You know me better than anyone else. I am sure you know that even though I can't express it, I do feel it.

I was sixteen when I grew out of the teenage hate period and realized how special you were. During that period, I said things to hurt you. Yet one day, I stopped feeling all the anger as a teenager and knew how lucky I was to have such a great mother. I feel sorry for all the ways I must have hurt you. I wanted to tell you so many times that I didn't mean it, and I was just taking the stress of being a kid out on you. You were the one person who kept telling me I was wonderful, even when I was acting like a spoiled brat. I never told you how sorry I was. But I did start doing the dishes every night. I think you noticed and understood what my actions meant.

Even now, I do the little things to tell you. I buy you presents for your birthday and for Christmas. I buy you little presents every now and then just to tell you in my own way, thank you. When I was a child, you did the same for me—just to show how special I was. I see that things come full circle.

I want you to know that I appreciate everything you have ever done for me. I love you. I want you to know that if I had to name my favorite person in all the world, I would name you. I want you to know that tears come to my eyes just thinking that one day you will no longer be in my life.

Especially, I want you to know that you are my hero. I look at my actions and I tell myself that I want to be like my mother. I aim to be as strong, kind, thoughtful, and giving as you are. You are my quiet hero who never takes credit, but who always puts her family first. My mother who cares about people so much, it hurts.

My greatest wish is that you realize how much I strive to be a strong individual who is kind, caring, and helpful. The good person I have become is all because of you.

My second fear is the sadness of having to live my life without you someday. But that fear disappears, too, because I know you will always be with me. You have given me a deep happiness, courage, and inner strength that are within me forever. Although sometimes I falter and fail, I find strength thinking of you. Thank you for being part of my life and for being who you are.

Your forever-grateful daughter, Shelley

A Tribute to You, Mom

Pain is a given; suffering is a choice.
GERRI SCHARF, *Florida*

Dear Mom,
Any woman who has children knows that not only is being a mom the hardest thing in life, but it's also the most rewarding. What a dichotomy.

This is a tribute to you, Mom.

Although most of us believe that our moms are the best, I know that you are the best person you can be. At your age of eighty-one, I'm lucky to still have you in my life. Although you suffer from emphysema and leukemia, you are the ultimate caregiver to everyone around you. Not only did you lose your firstborn child, my sister, a year ago, but you are generous enough to take care of my father, who is suffering from Alzheimer's.

How grateful I am. How lucky I am. How wealthy I am. And it doesn't have anything to do with currency. You are the most caring person one could ever have the honor to meet. You are another Mother Teresa. Best of all, you chose me to be one of your daughters.

We all have lessons to learn in every incarnation, but to have you be one of my teachers is more than a blessing. I humbly thank you, Mom, for being who you are and making me aware and enlightened to what really is important.

Pain is a given; suffering is a choice. Although we all have our tragedies, I know that losing a daughter is the most painful, and yet you continue to do God's work. Giving, giving, giving to help all others.

I am so proud to have you as my mother, and I respectfully thank you for being you. I love you and always will.

Gerri

Despite My Hearing Loss,
You Taught Me to Sing

Never was I forbidden to do something because I was hearing impaired. You taught teamwork when you encouraged the other girls to always explain things. I hardly ever felt left out.

CYNTHIA JEAN HEIDECKER, *Texas*

Dear Mom,

Mother, your aim in life for me was to be well educated, to be brought up to have a respectable reputation, and to work for the very best that life offers. You were a lady of many talents. A registered nurse, a dental assistant, a policewoman, and a secretary. Being a career mother, you still found time to be a Girl Scout leader, a room mother, a part of the PTA board. You stayed fully involved in my education.

As a young child, I had my tonsils removed and slowly lost my hearing. Mom, you didn't want this to set me back, so you made a deal with my teachers. It was agreed you would put a blank recording tape in my coat pocket each morning. Upon arrival at school, my teachers would tactfully remove the tape, place it in their recorders, and record the full day's lessons. Then they'd return the tape to my coat pocket. After your busy workday, you'd arrive home and head straight to the tape and the typewriter. You'd listen and type out the entire day's worth of lessons so I could read them while you fixed supper. Lip-reading all day has its barriers; reading what you typed helped me pick up what I failed to catch in lip-reading. This took place all through sixth, seventh, eighth, ninth, and a half semester of tenth grade. At that time, I got transferred to Omaha School for the Deaf in Nebraska where I learned to be a leader and developed a social life. However, I lacked nothing educationwise due to you, Mom, and your dedication to my successful future.

Teaching, communicating, sharing feelings, learning right from wrong because of your police training, learning to be a respectable lady in dress as well as in attitude, and getting an education were the top priorities you set. You were my teacher, mentor, and best friend.

I wasn't treated differently than the other girls. I have memories of Girl Scout camping trips on which you taught me to sing even with a hearing loss. Never was I forbidden to do something because I was hearing impaired. You taught teamwork when you encouraged the other girls to always explain things. I hardly ever felt left out.

Mom, you made me use my eyes since my ears were limited. You taught me at a young age to work. I attended babysitting courses and had more babysitting jobs than my hearing friends because my eyes had full contact with the kids most of the time. When putting them to bed, I checked them often. Hearing kids relied on sound and didn't always know what the kids were doing or where the kids were. You tirelessly taught me, from sunrise to sunset. I had piano lessons, clarinet lessons, and baton-twirling lessons. I was a drum majorette at Barr Junior High and Grand Island High in Nebraska.

When you and Dad got a divorce, we became more like sisters. Struggling financially, we rented a small apartment that consisted of a tiny kitchen, a living room, and one bedroom. The bathroom was shared among other tenants. You and I shared our bed, snuggling together, chatting about our day and our future plans.

In my senior year, you were diagnosed with breast cancer. Our close relationship remained and you taught me to stand on my own two feet. I went on to college to be the best I could be. Since education was a top priority in your life, you saw me graduate with honors on May 31, 1970. On July 25 that year, my dear Mother, you left this world with the peace of knowing you taught me well and had no fear that I was lacking in anything.

Thirty-two years later, I thank you often for being a wonderful, caring mother who believed there was nothing I couldn't do. Your high expectations and strong motivation made me what I am today: a wife of thirty years, a mother of two grown daughters, a grandmother of two precious grandchildren, a Bible-class teacher, a devotional writer, a camp teacher, and a workshop instructor. Even though I struggle with severe lupus, because of your strength and example, I have been able to cope with all that life has dealt me.

Thanks, Mom, for raising me to know there is nothing in life too great that we cannot learn. You were my inspiration and provided footsteps for me to follow.

Sincerely, Cindy

For Mom on Your Fiftieth Birthday

*Through the highs and lows of bipolar disorder and the
ups and downs of a learning disability, you were there for
me and you supported me.*

ROCHELLE FLYNN, *Ohio*

Dear Mom,

You have spent all of these years climbing and striving with
determination and diligence to be the best person you can be.
Your life has been an uncharted course that you have desperately hoped would make sense—one day.

Well, that day has arrived; you have reached the summit.
From your vantage point, you can reflect on and assess your
journey thus far. Have you accomplished all of your dreams?
Have you successfully nurtured your family? Have you
made a difference in this life?

As your daughter, I can honestly tell you that you have.
You have grown into the person you were meant to be, while
simultaneously raising your three children to be the people
they are meant to be. You have created and maintained a ful-

filling marriage, lasting friendships, and beautiful memories. You have been selfless and kind, and I envy your successes.

Most of all, though, I am proud to call you my mother. I sincerely hope that I can match your accomplishments. You are one of a kind, and I don't believe anyone can dream of reaching such potential as perfectly as you have done. Our relationship has had an amazing impact on my life. For that reason, I know you have made a difference to every individual you have encountered.

Despite all that you have done to make my life easy, we both know that it hasn't been. I don't blame you for my problems and I know how hard you tried to solve them for me. Through the highs and lows of bipolar disorder and the ups and downs of a learning disability, you were there for me and you supported me. Fortunately, I've been able to find peace within myself, but your contribution to my sanity means more to me than that peace ever could.

Your daughter, Rochelle

Thanks for Your Nurturing

At that moment, all eyes were on me, but yours weren't filled with doubt anymore; they were filled with amazement. With the determination, courage, and confidence that you had for me, I made it.

ELISABETH A. KIPKA, *Minnesota*

Dear Mom,

"God blessed me when he sent you" are a few words to express the way I feel about you. These words have had meaning all of my life even before my car accident on May 25, 2001, but I never knew the full extent of them. I know there were hard times when I was disrespectful and rude. I can never take back those times. I wish I could take back the hurt and pain I caused you, but there will always remain a bit of pain deep down in my heart. Since my car accident, there have been extremely tough times and you have always been by my side.

While being put in a neck collar and backboard, all I

could think was that I wanted you with me. As I was lying on a bed in the ER, I heard the pain and sadness in your voice, which I'll never forget. You sat there for hours with me, which was the best support of all.

The time after my accident seemed to be the most sensitive period for me, so I will always remember the ways in which you cared for me. When you washed my hair, you used such love and compassion in doing so, especially since you had to gently remove my neck collar. That was scary for both of us, but you never complained while doing it.

You tried to make the transition easier for me when the fuss of my accident calmed down. Even though there were the black-and-blue bruises on my body, there was so much more going on in the inside—the emotional injuries. My nightmares and daymares kept you from your sleep. You were determined to get me the best care and treatment, always providing motherly nurturing.

During all of this, you encouraged me to go back to school for my senior year, even though I didn't want to. It was rough, and many people doubted me right from the start. You encouraged me every day that I could make it. I tried so hard both physically and academically for months and was proud of myself for how much I accomplished.

We were both hoping I would get well, but I never expected the back pain to get worse. Not only have you gone with me to many specialists and surgeons, but you also brought my schoolwork to me when I was homebound. You've been so great with all the insurance people, lawyers, and teachers.

Thank you so much! You've made sacrifices for me during this rough time; you've dealt with me when I've been irritable and discouraged. My heart grieves whenever I act crabby toward you and I'm sorry.

There is a picture on our wall that says, "People need loving the most when they deserve it the least." The road has been long, but with you by my side, I can go on.

The proudest moment was when they read my name off at graduation and I was pushed in the wheelchair to get my diploma. At that instant, all eyes were on me, but yours weren't filled with doubt anymore; they were filled with amazement. With the determination, courage, and confidence that you had for me, I made it.

Thank you for being there for me. No matter when I do get well, my love for you continues to grow each and every day. I will always love you and always remember the love you've shown.

Love, Beth

The Woman Inside Me

I'm discovering the woman who lives inside you. At the same time, I think you're beginning to see the woman inside me.

ANNE WARREN SMITH, *Oregon*

Dear Mother,

Here you are, still going strong at ninety-six. I'm so glad you're with me still. These last years have been hard ones. It's not easy for a daughter to be such a busybody in her mother's life. I'm learning how it costs us—mother and daughter. We do well for a while; then we stumble. You go back to being the critical mother and tell me I'm doing everything wrong. I turn back into a teenager and tell you to stop criticizing me.

Lately, however, you put your hand in mine more readily—you've come to trust that I won't let you fall. You've stopped gasping when I steer the wheelchair too close to the wall. We make jokes in the restroom as you cling to the wheelchair, willing your knees to lock, trying not to sink back onto the toilet seat. We're figuring out that we don't go on forever being able or efficient or clever. Instead, we do the best we can.

At one time you laid out my dresses; today, I lay out yours. Once you cut up my meat and helped me climb the stairs. Today, I make a casserole that's easy to chew and I support you taking those shaky steps from the wheelchair to the car. When I was little and had a bad dream, you turned on the lights and told me a story. Last night, when you told me you were afraid to die, I did the only things I knew how to do: I turned on the lights and got out the baby pictures.

We've done most of our traveling as a mother and a daughter. Today, our roles blur—and I like that. We've blurred ourselves into two women! Side by side, helping each other walk this new road, I'm discovering the woman who lives inside of you—a woman who adds substance to the picture of "my mother." Sometimes I even see the child and the teenager you once were. At the same time, I think you're beginning to see the woman inside me.

I intend to remember these feelings with my own daughters—if only I can live a long life, just as you have. I know that I, too, will someday need help in ways I don't expect. My daughters—these grown women—will extend their hands to me, and I, myself a grown woman, will take them.

I didn't know all this until recently. What a gift you've given me. I'm so happy we can celebrate this birthday together. Happy Birthday.

Love, Anne

By Your Hands

Yet you still wanted me back. I'm finally old enough to realize that you will always want me back because that's the way mothers are.

MARY ELLEN SHORES, *North Carolina*

Dear Mama,

It may have happened while I was washing dishes, folding clothes, or writing a letter, but suddenly, without me even noticing it, my hands had been transformed into yours.

The closely cut fingernails, slightly enlarged knuckles, and even the same dryness crying out for a therapeutic lotion were now mine along with the fair complexion and freckles. I stopped what I was doing at the time to stare at my hands in disbelief as though something supernatural had just occurred. Whether I liked the resemblance was not an issue for I could not change reality. I began to think about all the ways your hands have molded me to be the woman I now am.

With your hands, you held me and cared for me when I was a baby.

As your first child, I know I was special to you, though I don't know if it was more disappointing to realize that you would not be naming me Jeffrey James, or that I was bald and had a deformed lip—a far cry from the Gerber baby you had imagined. Not only that, but when my hair came in a year later, it would be red, an unimaginable color in an all-brunette family. Several years ago when you admitted I looked more like you than my sisters did, I wondered if the resemblance made you smile.

In your hands, you held up books that would open my imagination.

Though you never considered yourself a scholar, your decision to read to me caused me to fall in love with books and has helped to set the course of my life. I don't remember what you read other than nursery rhymes, but reading has always been something I have loved and I can credit you for that.

By putting your hands together, you showed me how to pray.

My earliest memory is kneeling by my bed with hands folded, eyes shut, reciting prayers. As I grew in my knowledge of God and was compelled to follow a path different from yours, I knew my decision would create a problem for us. And yet if I did not walk the path shown to me, I would be doing something far worse. It's important for a mother to teach her child about that which is most dear to her. It's because I have strong convictions, like yours, that we have never been able to settle this matter.

Your hands kneaded the dough, and cut out cookies.

How fortunate I have been to have a mother who knew how to cook! All those pies and cookies we made represent a lot of what was good about my childhood. Though we won awards for our baked goods, the memory is better than any blue ribbon.

With your hands you could take whatever you had to create anything.

I learned resourcefulness from you, even though I know you wished you hadn't lived that lesson the way you always have. But you became good at turning one piece of clothing into another, a sheet into a costume or curtains, scraps of cloth into decorations.

The hands that made crafts to become gifts for others were yours.

Not only did you make do with anything with which you had to work, but also you never allowed your lack of money to keep you from giving gifts. You simply created gifts out of whatever you could find.

With your hands you made clothes for yourself and your children.

Your sewing skills won you awards and gave you the

ability to create outfits for your daughters that would match yours. Wearing the green jacket you made for yourself allows me to wonder what you may have looked like when you were young and free.

By your hands, you prepared meal after meal.

We depended on you for your cherry dessert, the perfect piecrusts, and the many salads and desserts you came up with to take to school events and picnics. It never occurred to me how much work you did, just that you would be there to do it.

Holding your hands, we could safely cross any street.

You must have been praying when we tried to cross those busy streets in Chicago during our first family vacation. You wanted to give us the chance to see the world, though, so you helped us across the street.

Your hands clapped at my performances and accomplishments.

Piano recitals, band concerts, 4-H fashion shows, and even a cherry-queen pageant. There you were, my biggest fan. Graduations were more difficult because I was closer to leaving the nest with each step. Maybe that was why my wedding was most difficult of all.

Your hands waved good-bye.

It must have bothered you to leave me at Michigan State University, as big as it is. There was a time after I declared what I believed in and how I was going to live my life that I wondered if you had waved good-bye to me for the last time. But your mother's love would not allow it.

Your hands were open, ready for hello.

Even after everything I have put you through—running off to Denver with twenty-five dollars and a backpack, turning a two-week vacation into a two-year stay; taking a job in Maryland and ending up in California still seeking my path; not taking the journalist position I was finally offered in the Colorado mountains because I didn't have money to get there and was too afraid to ask for more; having a wedding so foreign that you couldn't accept it—yet you still wanted me back. I'm finally old enough to realize that you will *always* want me back because that's the way mothers are.

Your hands have always reached out to those in your community.

The example you gave me when you made endless plates of cookies and sent cards to people for every occasion, but especially get-well cards, has served as a standard by which I can hope to live.

In your hands is a mother's love for your children and grandchildren.

A mother's love is that constant affection that goes beyond changing a sick child's bed or cleaning up messes when she has no energy left, especially in the middle of the night.

You probably dreamed of a more glamorous existence, and I know you have wanted that for me. But fame and fortune don't equal love, especially the kind that covers a multitude of sins. And well-manicured, painted fingernails just aren't your style. Your example of caring for others has helped me to serve my family in a way that formal education could never accomplish. I'm sorry it has taken me so long to realize that.

By your hands, another generation goes forward.

Getting married and having my own family has been possible because I watched you do it and knew I wanted it, too. I just didn't want it as badly as you did or as soon. I judged you for making that your primary goal, when there were so many other possibilities. I hope you can forgive me for that, but I didn't understand motherhood at the time. When all is said and done, I know I will value my family as much as you have because that's what a mother does.

Your hands are more familiar to me now, for they resemble my own.

I've now held my own babies, shared my love for reading, and continued to teach them about God's love. I still bake the bread, make the cookies, and become resourceful creating gifts, clothing, and meals out of whatever I can find. I walk hand in hand with my little boys and cheer them on during soccer games and music performances. I haven't had to wave good-bye to them yet, but that day will come. Then I hope and pray that what you taught me and what I've taught them will help them make good decisions.

I'm still learning to be aware of the community and care for another's need more than my own. Someday, if I live long enough, I may have a grandchild who will want to know her great-grandmother. Then I will stretch out my worn, bony fingers with crackling dry skin and say, "I want to tell you all about her. Look, child, at my hands."

Love, Mary Ellen

Embracing Sweet Sorrow

I have been carrying the emotions and sentiment around with me for years; therefore, the letter itself was both easy and very hard for me to write. My mother's depression is such a hard thing for all involved to deal with. After completing the letter, I felt a sense of letting go. I realize she has to help herself.

THERESE ANDERSON, *North Carolina*

I lifted a leaf and discovered a monarch's cocoon that re-sembles a waxy, jade vase. So enthralled by the caterpillar's transformation, I took it home to watch it emerge into a beautiful butterfly.

The next day, I noticed through the transparent chrysalis how the butterfly was struggling to free itself. I watched as it couldn't force its body past a certain point. Believing something was terribly wrong, I snipped the chrysalis open. Though the monarch entered the outside world easily, its body was frail and its wings were small and shriveled. I waited patiently for the wings to bloom fully. Yet instead of attaining its natural proportions, the butterfly remained weak and unable to fly.

With great effort, every butterfly must pass through its cocoon. It's nature's way of forcing fluid through the abdomen into its wings—a necessary process. My sympathetic cut of this monarch's cocoon short-circuited that step, resulting in an inhumane act.

As if we are butterflies emerging from our cocoons, we often feel restless dealing with the stickiness of sorrow we feel in our hearts. Panicking, we thrust forward in an attempt to break free of our sadness. Once we become exhausted with our efforts, we hopelessly fall back to shed pitiful tears. And we ask, "Why me? Will I ever get over this sorrow I feel?"

As if it were yesterday, I remember sitting on a bench, sobbing in front of a big oak tree. I had just moved with my fiancé into a house that needed major renovations. I was going through a merger in my job, and a slew of letters for this Project were coming in from women all over the world. I had expected I'd be able to leave my job and devote myself fully to Letters from the Heart™. I also expected that a publisher would pick up this Project quickly, that our house would be completed in six months, and that living with my fiancé would be grand.

In reality, I was stomping my feet loudly on the ground—frustrated that nothing was going according to plan. My entire world went into a tailspin. After two years, our house was still in disarray, my fiancé and I were going through many trials of living together, and I was still working full-time while this Project began to blossom. The more I forced myself to skip the process of growth that had to occur, the more frustrated I became. After much inner turmoil, I finally exhausted myself into letting go of my plan and peacefully accepting where I was at the moment.

As Rainer Maria Rilke profoundly states in *Letters to a Young Poet,* "Don't search for the answers, which could not be given you now, because you would not be able to live them, and the point is, to live everything. Live the questions now." After much discipline, compromise, and sacrifice, I did get all the things I'd planned for. Yet all the challenges and the powerful lessons learned along the way made me appreciate them so much more. I now understand why a butterfly must struggle.

Most of the stories in this chapter show both peace and sorrow within one letter. Some women protect themselves from the overwhelming pull exerted by their mothers while others live their truth regardless of tradition and their mothers' wishes. And some finally realize that their mothers are a godsend—after letting go of the way they think a mother should be.

We trust that all of us have our bridges to cross before we can touch the rainbow on the other side. It's our collective voice of sorrow sweetly calling, "I have lived through this," that enables us to receive the rapture of joy.

Separated by Tradition

One part of you resented the relationship I had with Alam, but the other part of you—the mother concerned with the well-being of her only child—approved of it.

SHARMILA, *India*

Mom,

I am writing this letter, sitting hundreds of miles away from you, watching the twilight stealthily creeping into the kitchen and the milk boiling on the gas burner. A little while ago, I dialed home, and you picked up the telephone and mumbled a sleepy "Hello!" (I guess I had interrupted your evening siesta.) The thrill of hearing your voice after such a long time rendered me speechless. I closed my eyes and instantly, as if by some miracle, I was in your room and could clearly visualize you sitting on the couch and speaking to me. I slowly put the receiver down and wept.

After some time, I dialed again (though I had tried hard not to), and instantly you were there at the other end, sounding somewhat irritated. Then suddenly, there was complete silence. However, you had not put the receiver down, for I could hear your gentle breathing. Perhaps you had guessed who was calling.

Mom, do you remember when I was small, you used to tell me, "Don't think that I cannot see through your pretensions." God has gifted mothers with a sixth sense! I did not believe it then, but I do now.

Mom, hearing you, I was suddenly flooded with memories of home, of my room with the madhabilata creepers in the window and the long verandah in the west where you used to oil my curly tresses every Saturday afternoon.

I longed to go back, though I knew deep in my heart that the door to that house was closed to me forever. The day I had done the unthinkable thing by eloping with Alam, I had died in the eyes of my father. Father was a die-hard Hindu and I knew he would never pardon me for marrying a Muslim. No, I don't blame him a bit for that. He had only acted according to his own set of principles.

I still remember that night clearly, down to the minutest detail. I knew that it was going to be my last night in the house, and accordingly, I was packing my bags and pretending to prepare for college the next day when you entered my room. Immediately I was tense, though I tried to look casual and composed.

"Want to say anything?" I had asked, avoiding eye contact. You did not reply. Instead, you looked at me. "When are you going to college tomorrow?"

"I have to be there by eight. The function will start at ten." I hesitated a bit and asked, "Why?"

"No, nothing. I was asking just like that."

Then you did a strange thing. You opened the gold chain that you were wearing and put it around my neck. "What is all this?" I was shaking with a sudden nervousness. So had you guessed my plans—that the next day I would run away from home with Alam on the pretext of going to college?

"Wear it for the farewell. You had been wanting to wear this for a long time." And pausing for a while, you looked straight into my eyes and said, "Take care." You sounded perfectly normal, but I was very much shaken.

Now, when I sit back and analyze the events, I realize that you had very well realized my intentions. Still, you didn't stop me. Perhaps you had realized in your own life that just matching religious backgrounds doesn't make a marriage work. What a wife needs most from her husband is his love. Without that, everything else appears meaningless.

Your father had arranged your marriage after ensuring that everything about the both of you was in place: the caste, the social status of both the families, and even the horoscopes. However, what happened ultimately?

Father's life revolved around his company and his lover, Ranjini, whom we used to call Jinimasi in our childhood. Of course, at that time we were not aware of her real status. To us, she was just one of the many aunties who worked in Father's office.

Even at that early age, I could make out that Father rarely had time or need for you. Like a Barbie doll, you were just a showpiece in his life. I remember the day you first met Alam in the shopping plaza and how the three of us had gone to a nearby café where we had chatted for a long time over coffee, cheese sandwiches, and ice cream.

Slowly, over a period of time and with successive interactions, you had started liking him. When you sensed our growing intimacy, I guess you were of two minds. One part of you, the practical one, resented the relationship. The other half of you, the mother concerned with the well-being of her only child, approved of it—the mother who had realized Alam was capable of giving a daughter all those things that she herself had been deprived of in her own marital life. I guess that is why you did not stand in my way that night.

Initially after my marriage, we were too engrossed with each other to feel the absence of anyone or anything. Life moved on and we with it, leaving the past behind. Eight months flew by.

Yesterday evening, we returned home from the doctor—

I'd been feeling weak and complaining of loss of appetite for the last few days. Alam and I were going to have a baby. Instantly, I remembered you.

I yearned to pick up the telephone and scream with joy, "Mother, I am going to be a mother, too!" Nevertheless, I held myself back. I did not want Father to find out that I had spoken to you and trouble you. I fought against myself the entire day and finally decided to talk to you. But when you picked up the telephone, I was unable to utter even a single word.

Hence, I am writing this letter. After I have finished and before Alam returns home, I will tear it into a thousand pieces and throw them into the air from our tenth-floor balcony. And as I watch them fly away to unknown destinations, I would love to think that someday, one of them will reach home and touch your feet as you stand on the sun-kissed terrace, staring into the empty sky and thinking of me. Maybe today, maybe tomorrow.

Love, Sharmila

A Missed Opportunity

Now, as my time marches on, I have come to realize what an opportunity I missed. The opportunity to get to know you woman to woman rather than mother to child.

MAUREEN HADZICK, NEW YORK

Dear Mom,

If I could turn back the hands of time, where would I stop? A month, a year, two years before that dreadful day in June that took you away forever.

I think back now to those two years after your stroke—the two years that you spent in my care. You were in a wheelchair, paralyzed on your right side. I was a young mother with a four-year-old and a two-year-old. My days revolved around physical therapy, doctors' visits (yours or the children's), and housecleaning, making dinners, and picking up toys. Handicapped parking didn't exist and many friends were decidedly uncomfortable around your being in a wheelchair. I often felt tired and resentful about having a mother who couldn't take care of herself.

Now, as my time marches on, I have come to realize what an opportunity I missed. The opportunity to get to know you woman to woman rather than mother to child. The opportunity to understand you as a person, not just my mother. To sit down with a cup of coffee and talk about life. Your life. The life that ended before I was smart enough or mature enough to realize just how short life can be.

I imagine us sitting over that cup of coffee, asking all the questions that now will remain unanswered. I want to know what it felt like to leave your home and family in Ireland and come to a strange, unknown land. I want to know if you were ever so afraid that your heart seemed as if it would pound out of your chest. I want to know where you met Dad and when and where he asked you to marry him. Did you ever feel like life was so much that you wanted to walk out the front door and keep on walking? And when did you cry? I don't remember ever seeing you cry, you were so strong. Oh, the questions I have could fill a lifetime.

Always in my heart, Maureen

Please Wake Up from Your Depression

Your own survival has become dependent on the medication and painkillers that have numbed your very soul to the point, I fear, of no return.

THERESE ANDERSON, *North Carolina*

Mother,

I am your eldest child. I have been your truest confidant, your best friend, and your worst enemy. Together, we have spent endless hours rehashing the old times, the good times, the scary times, and the most horrendous of times. I have shared more of your life than any of my siblings and any of your friends. I came to you for advice, encouragement, unconditional love, and, at times, money. You came to me for respect, trust, unconditional love, and, at times, advice.

I write this today to honor the woman you once were, the woman who dared to dream, the woman who dared to take chances, the woman who dared to love. I honor the free spirit that you once held within you. Though I know the years would have naturally eroded some of this, you deteriorated at lightning speed before my very eyes. I don't have the knowledge or power to stop you.

Today, you are an empty shell of the person I once knew, looked up to, and admired. I understand that the depression is not entirely of your own making. There is a chemical imbalance that drags you down into that black hole where you now live.

You allow others to help you dig deeper down to where only the lowest dregs of life survive. Your own survival has become dependent on the medication and painkillers that have numbed your very soul to the point, I fear, of no return.

I don't know exactly when the transformation began or where it will lead. It frightens me. I'm afraid for you, but I think I'm even more afraid for myself. My being contains most of your character traits, your sense of morals, and your looks. I am afraid because I no longer want to become the woman whom I most admired as a child. I don't want to emulate you or your existence. I want to continue to walk in the light. I want to see the good in the world.

Mother, you are the woman whom I will always love the most, the one I will always love unconditionally and forever, no matter what. But I miss the "you" that once was. I cherish the memories of the woman who taught me to dance in the living room. I treasure the times we laughed together at the silly jokes only we could share. I embrace the arguments we had in my teenage years when I was trying so hard to stretch my wings and you were trying to keep me safe while I did so. I hold these moments dear to me because they were real.

I choose to think of the present as unreal—an impossibility that life could take such a cruel turn of events and that the simple act of just living and just life could destroy a person's very being. I find it unbelievable that the one person who means the most to me is incapable of enjoying even the simplest of pleasures on a daily basis. I dare to hope that this is just another phase of life, or a bad dream. I dare to hope that someday you will awaken from this nightmare.

Sometimes when I look deeply into your eyes, I can see the shadow of who you once were and I know that somewhere she still exists. Sometimes when you smile I can see the sheer joy of life that you once held. Some days you speak with the wisdom only a truly full person could know. But most of the time, lately, there is just a drab, lifeless expression on your face, in your voice, and in your aura.

You have given so much of yourself to me over the years. I wish I could give you some back, but to do so would be to remove my very soul. You have taught me so much over the years. I wish I could teach you how to be happy. I owe you my very existence. I wish I could repay you with the will to live.

Very sincerely,
Your daughter Therese

Precious Memories

What's so important about a silly old baby book?
JUDITH C. ISSETTE, *North Carolina*

My dearest Mother,
Some might ask me, "What's so important about a silly old baby book?" Even I must say with regret that it wasn't important to me when I was five years old, or even when I was twenty. It's such a shame that our memories start so late in life. I had too many other interests to pursue, but it was important to you, Mother. You hung on to it for nearly sixty years, protecting it and preserving it as a legacy of my first years on this earth. I wish I had left a better legacy for my children to someday look back at their book and say, "Look at how much my mother loved me."

As I look through that old book today, it's important to me now. And the thing I love most about it is that it's a part of you, Mother. We are bonded together for life through that old, faded, crumbling book of memories. A book I know you lovingly wrote just for me. Thank you, Mother.

All my love always,

Your daughter Judith

I'm Not Ready

My myth is beginning to tatter, that you and Dad will re-main ageless to care for me.

SHERRI GOODALL, *Oklahoma*

Dear Mom,

This morning I noticed your arms.

We sat across from each other in your citrus yellow kitchen having a cup of coffee. As you lifted your cup, I noticed your doughy arm, the skin loose at the back. Your wrist had lost its definition, like the arm of a newborn that folds into its hand. Your elbow was fleshy, hiding the bone. Blue veins rose up out of the tops of your hands, peeking through the brown age spots.

I had this crazy thought: "What if I connected all the spots?"

Your fingernails were flawless pink ovals, manicured yesterday. I complimented you on your always-perfect nails. Then I closed my eyes and repeated the litany that had become rote: *My good fortune in having you and Dad alive and in reasonably good mental and physical health—still "verti-*

*cal" as I liked to phrase it—both in the winter of your lives . . .
your full and serene lives.*

I opened my eyes and saw Dad, his arms still sinewy and
muscular, reading the newspaper. His arms that built and re-
paired countless toys, appliances, and model railroads over
the years. They wrote on blackboards, penned books, and
drove us across country so many hot summers to vacation
and learn. You would sit in the front seat, unpin your blouse,
crank down all the car windows, and fan yourself. Dad re-
quired strong arms to shovel away the Colorado snow forty
winters ago.

I noticed a slight tremor as he held the paper.

I shut my eyes and recite the litany again. I am the baby
and the only daughter. I am the one you take care of. My
myth is beginning to tatter, that you and Dad will remain
ageless to care for me. I must ask the questions. You must
have the answers. But now the sequence is off kilter. I'm not
ready to be the caretaker.

I know before I leave today we must have the conversation regarding your move into the retirement facility. I'm
prepared with pamphlets, photos, glowing accolades, and a
hundred reasons why it will be better for you and Dad to
move while you still can enjoy your freedom and health, yet
have fewer obligations to cook, clean, drive, and care for a
home. Neither of you is ecstatic about the idea.

I will gently remind you of Dad's failing memory, his getting lost in areas he's been driving for thirty years, your fainting episode when Dad revived you with CPR, and your pacemaker.

Then I think of your incredible memory, much better than mine: your recall of minutia, telephone numbers and addresses from sixty years ago, how Aunt Gussie is related, and all those weird relatives in Canada that only you understand. You remember the guest list from my wedding thirty-nine years ago and who sent what for presents. You remember cute things my children said as infants and which hairdo I sported twenty-five years ago. You remember coming to visit me at college and meeting my boyfriend/husband and even what we ate for dinner that night. You remember the first visit of my future in-laws to our house one summer over forty years ago and what my future mother-in-law was wearing, her purse, and her shoes. You tell me about meeting your husband (of almost sixty-nine years) for the first time at a sweet-sixteenth birthday party in 1933. You remember the dress you wore and what he, my father, wore.

Dad is going to refill his teacup. His hand shakes as he pours and hot water splashes on the kitchen floor. You and I exchange a glance, and you barely shake your head as if you are reading my thoughts.

I look at my own arms. They haven't scrubbed the steps

(up one day, down the next) or washed the walls or baked the cookies (legendary cookies that all five of your grandchildren still consider manna from heaven) or carried the worries that your arms have. My arms have just begun to cradle grandchildren; they are still shapely and taut. Yours have cradled great-grandchildren. My arms haven't let go of loved ones. Sadly, yours have.

I look at your arms again. They are carefully opening a photo album. You are lost in your memories; a gentle smile plays across your face.

Maybe we will talk tomorrow.

Your daughter, Sherri

Will I Always Be Your Little Girl?

I let go of you, Mama, knowing you had moved beyond this plane of life. Did you find your own blue welcome mat and an encouraging nod from the teacher at the door?

SHERRI WEINBERGER, *Arizona*

Dear Mama,

"You'll always be my little girl," you whispered as we entered the kindergarten room. Other children were already there. Some were playing by themselves or in small groups. Whole Christmas catalogs full of toys beckoned us. A few children, thumbs in mouths and eyes wide, clung to their mothers' skirts while the moms tried to gently peel them off. One boy wailed a liquid scream into his kneeling mother.

Your mouth twisted into a sort of wistful, sad smile. "Honey, if you don't want to stay, we can go home."

Go home? Why would I want to do that?

The small, white-haired teacher introduced herself. "Welcome to school. My name is Mrs. Harms. Would you like to join the other children playing with the big blocks on the blue mat?"

I looked at her in wonder. You would have told me that these toys were for other children. Mrs. Harms nodded yes in encouragement.

Without a look back, I walked to the blue mat.

When you told the story, you always concluded by telling me how I didn't even say good-bye to you. I think you wanted me to be the fearful, wailing child and you resented that I wasn't.

On November 22, I just held your hand, trying to ward off the fear of your next step. And like I had so long ago, you left without saying good-bye, moving off into a world that beckoned you, and in which you belonged.

I let go of you, Mama, knowing you had moved beyond this plane of life. Did you find your own blue welcome mat and an encouraging nod from the teacher at the door? You'll always be my mama. I hope I'll always be your little girl.

Love, Sherri

Leaving Shame Behind

Writing this letter opened my heart to be able to see my mother not only as my parent but also as a woman who came to adulthood already wounded. I realize she did the best she could with what she had at the time.

ANNA CLINE, *Pennsylvania*

In the movie *The Man without a Face*, Mel Gibson plays a retired teacher who is severely burned on one side of his face. He isolates himself in a beautiful house on top of a cliff to avoid further humiliation and mockery by others in town. Regardless of his hiding, people talk about him as if he were a monster. They shame him and devalue him as a human being. He feels ashamed of himself.

Then Mel Gibson's character reveals his vulnerability as he shows a young boy how to overcome his struggle with the

English language—and his struggle with himself. Both characters uncover and transform their shame by teaching each other the value and beauty of their own beings.

Shame has deep-rooted beginnings. Many of us can see the dark reflections of ourselves mirrored in these characters and can remember incidents of being ashamed as children. I vividly recall when my brother was diagnosed with schizophrenia and was branded an outcast by others. I felt the excruciating pain of my brother's struggle, observing how each family member dealt with the complexities of his disease and the many faces of humiliation that accompany it. I also recall a time as a teenager when boys called me "sewer rat" because of my awkwardness. I would come home after school and sob outwardly to my mother that I was ugly. Even though my mother would tell me that I was beautiful, my self-worth was lost in the perceptions of others.

As others inflict upon us unkind words and ignorant statements, we inflict shame on ourselves—shame that might still be very much alive within us long after those people are gone. We might secretly loathe a part of ourselves that robs us of the whole person we could be. Our society pressures us about our skin color, sexuality, religion, appearance, and inability to measure up to the expectations of others. When we succumb to this negativity, there's no difference between the imprisonment of our souls and the physical bars of prison. Wisdom comes from knowing that we can break away from what others think and discover the best part of ourselves.

Beckie Miller, whose letter appears in this chapter, expressed her experience with this insight: "If we allow a painful and difficult situation in our lives to continue without doing what is right to try to prevent its continuance, the person responsible becomes more powerful, and we in turn become not just their victim, but also a victim of ourselves and our fears. My sisters and I are no longer victims of our father's abuse. We are no longer in bondage to the shame by keeping silent. We are no longer victims, but survivors."

Many of the daughters who wrote the letters in this chapter bear their mothers' shame as their own. What the little girl inside each of us seeks most is our mother's approval, love, and affection. Yet we quickly learn that we cannot expect from our mothers what they cannot give to themselves. It is only when we accept ourselves that we gain the validation we seek.

These writers are truly remarkable because of their courage to find their own identities in the midst of conflicting messages and unfortunate circumstances. We can't erase the families we are born into or control what others think of us. But we do have the ability to remove the veil and unleash the shattered images of ourselves. We realize that our heart-to-heart connection surpasses race, sexuality, or religion. It's the resolving of our differences that helps us restore wholeness within.

Overcoming Abuse

What could I have done differently to make you choose the light?

BECKIE A. MILLER, *Arizona*

Dear Mom,

I learned what it was like to lose you again in January of 1996. Your obituary read the stuff of standard, impersonal paragraphs attempting to capture someone's life in a few sentences. What your obituary did not say was that I, and your family, actually lost you long before death physically claimed you at fifty-six years old. Spiritually, death laid claim to you many years before after all the incredible hurt and pain you endured in your life, sapped your joy for living, and left you simply going through the motions, devoid of joy.

You were a wife at the tender age of fourteen and gave birth to seven children by the age of twenty-four—hardly more than a child yourself when I, your firstborn daughter, arrived. By today's standards, it's almost impossible to imagine a child married and bearing babies so young. It must have been challenging then, pregnant, marrying a military man, and moving far away from family and friends. I can't imagine totally how it must have been for you, especially when Grandma Billie died at forty-two, a victim of asphyxiation while she slept. I know she would have been there for you during the tragedies that followed, holding your hand, guiding you, and helping all of us.

A daughter never stops needing her mother, and though I lost you long before your death, I had always hoped I would find you again before you succumbed completely. You see, though you gave in to the darkness—living life without joy, seeking answers, or redemption, in the wrong place, for the wrong reasons—I still always hoped for your return someday. A return to the mom not so weighted down and heavily burdened.

What brought you to the darkness was your husband, our father. What he did to your four daughters, no father should ever do. But your lack of courage in prosecuting him—in leaving him—is what brought you such horrendous pain that it sapped your spirit and drained your essence. It began with only me, but insidiously spread like a horrid disease to each of us in turn, as he was allowed to get away with it.

I wish you could have shared the wonderful event in my life. Five years after your firstborn grandchild, Brian, was robbed and shot to death at the age of eighteen, I stood trembling with absolute joy as the doctor handed me your newest grandchild. It was a true miracle in itself—the experience of feeling absolute joy again. I believed after Brian died, I would not, could not, ever feel it. It was a beautiful rebirth to hold my daughter Kimberlie as tears of happiness rolled down my cheeks.

Oh, Mom, how I wished I could have shared my new daughter with you, as I shared my first daughter, Christie. How I hate that Kimberlie will never know her grandmother.

I was angry at you for a long time after your death and even before. Angry you gave up on life, angry that you could not help me endure the agony of my own mother's grief, angry that, despite the darkness life dealt you, you could not still see the beauty around the good. It is a choice to survive, Mom. Not an easy choice.

The truth is, it's a lot of hard work and a commitment, but worth it. Maybe one reason I did not give in to the darkness as you did was because of seeing what it stole from you, from all your family. In a roundabout way, you were a part of my remaining whole when my life shattered into a thousand pieces and my heart along with it. I was changed, profoundly, but managed to keep my basic self intact nonetheless.

Now I simply feel sadness for all that you have missed

and all that I will continue to miss. I do know you were with my sisters and me last year through the tremendously difficult trial we endured. We had to finally hold our father accountable for what he did and how he continued after your death to hurt our baby sister Cindy, your youngest who suffers with muscular dystrophy. You would have been so proud of how she held up, Mom. I know your strength—a strength you could not draw upon while alive. It helped give her the courage necessary to get through the trial and put him where he cannot hurt again.

When Beth and I visited your grave after one of the court hearings, we were emotionally exhausted and reaching out for comfort from our mother. I know you answered us in your own way. We could not have found your headstone in the fourteen inches of hardpack snow without the tiny, red rosebud showing us the way. It was barely sticking above ground, but in such sharp contrast to the sea of blinding whiteness surrounding it. It beckoned to us, just when we were ready to give up our search.

We carefully dug through the snow beneath and found the rosebud was bent straight upward from a stem of three fully blooming roses lying on your marker. It was your way of showing us you knew that we three sisters were caring for our baby sister and helping her endure this difficult chapter of her life and ours. Thank you for being there for us, for your message of love—your motherly arms reaching out to touch us when we needed them the most.

I am no longer angry with you, Mom. I have spent the anger, worked through my grief. I miss you, though; I always will. There is a bond between a mother and daughter, forged with the commonality of our feminism, our distinct journey in life of daughterhood and motherhood. It cannot be broken, just as the cord of birth can never be severed.

I always knew you loved me despite losing you to the shadows. I hope you know I always loved you, even when I withdrew to protect myself from your darkness. I clung tenderly to the cord, never far from you, never totally letting go. I still cling to it.

Love,
Your daughter Beckie

Loving You from My Prison Cell

Do you realize how far we've come? Seeing us together now, who would ever think that you once changed the locks to our house so I couldn't get in?

DANIELLE BARCHEERS, *California*

Dear Mom,

Do you realize how far we've come in our relationship? Seeing us together now, who would ever think that not even eight years ago, you changed the locks to our house so I couldn't get in because you were so afraid of me, or that I left home because I was afraid of you? Anyone who knows how we are now together would never guess that CPS [Child Protective Services] took me from you as a very small child because your boyfriend was molesting me and beating me? Or when I was fourteen, you had to put a lock on your bedroom door just to feel safe from me at night because I couldn't forgive you.

I can still remember the fights we had, as if they happened yesterday. I don't know what was worse—the blows I was taking or the blows I gave the first time I hit you back. Both hurt in many ways.

I can still hear our angry words used like swords to cut at each other's hearts. Sometimes I thought that was better than the silence between us. We could hardly speak to each other without a fight.

The world was an ugly, scary place for me, and I felt so cheated because I couldn't remember ever feeling safe. I couldn't remember ever having the freedom of childhood because mine was taken from me. I could never see past the tears and pain, the drugs, anger, violence, and confusion. I imagine that was a fog that was just as thick for you to try to see me through as it was for me to see you. I was so angry that I never stopped to wonder if the world was just as scary for you.

Look at us now. You are my mother and one of my best friends. I can talk to you, trust you, confide in you, depend on you, and laugh with you—all things I thought we'd never have. I've forgiven you for everything and even understand a lot about you. What I don't understand I accept, because I love you. What's done is done. It's all in the past and we've both grown so much since then. Believe it or not, I've forgiven myself.

You've shown me in so many ways that you've forgiven me and I thank God for that. We are so much alike, so I know it's harder for you to forgive yourself than others. It is so important that you do, though.

So much has happened between then and now with both of us, but we are making it. We are strong women, Mom. We can handle anything that comes our way. I'm just so grateful we have each other to help us along the way.

As for others who don't know us, they would never guess that one of the best relationships a mother and daughter could have is shared between people with our backgrounds. How ironic that the closest we've been is when we've been forced the farthest apart!

Now I sit here writing you this letter from my prison cell where I may spend the rest of my life, and I have to give a moment of thanks for being allowed the chance to say I love you and to hear those words back from you. These are words eight years ago I thought would never be exchanged between us.

I have to give thanks that I didn't realize too late just how much I need you in my life—that I am able to send this to you and say just how I feel. I love you, Mom.

Always your baby, Danielle

Understanding the Cycle

This anger and resentment steadily built until I turned fifty—until I awakened to the awareness that I had become my mother, that I was an alcoholic.

BARBARA HINKLE, *West Virginia*

Dear Mom,

I am now the age you were when you died—fifty-three. It's been twenty-three years. I've just visited your grave to place the annual Memorial Day plastic flowers that if you could see them, they would make you laugh. Such irony—we always made fun of plastic flowers.

For the first year after your death, I mourned. I would go to pick up the phone and suddenly realize that I had no mother to call. The second year I began to feel relief—especially on holidays. Because you were an alcoholic in and out of recovery, holidays were usually pretty gruesome. That second year, I began to realize that I no longer had to dread the dysfunctional attempts at celebrating Thanksgiving, Christmas, and birthdays.

As my adult life progressed and the inevitable challenges in relationships arose, I became increasingly resentful for being who I was—your daughter, the daughter of an alcoholic mother. All of my childhood and teenage memories were tied up in your drinking, and I became angrier and angrier at you. This anger and resentment steadily built until I turned fifty—until I awakened to the awareness that I had become my mother, that I was an alcoholic.

I think of you carefully planning an elaborate Christmas celebration, beginning with a few cocktails on Christmas Eve and ending with the Christmas tree being knocked over and presents thrown out into the snow. I think of the Christmas mornings as an adult when I woke up with a hangover and had to start the dreaded day with Bloody Marys. I think of my thirteenth birthday having to be cancelled by calling my friends to tell them the party was off because my mother had the flu. In reality, the house was decorated, the cake baked, and you were lying on the living-room couch passed out. I think of my best friend's grandfather's funeral that I missed because I passed out and didn't awaken in time.

How I hated you. I cast so much blame on you. It was your fault that I failed at two marriages; it was your fault that I had a poor self-image; it was your fault that I drank. But in these past three years of sobriety, I have learned a lot about us both. Instead of always blaming you, I am now at the point where I can thank you. I thank you for my love of books and music; I thank you for my openness to diversity; I thank you for my quick wit and dry sense of humor; I thank you for all the Christmases and birthdays that you wanted to make special.

I wish I could go to the phone and call you. I would tell you I understand that you never wanted to be an alcoholic, that I know you suffered horribly from the disease, and that I realize you could never move beyond it—it finally defeated you.

I would tell how blessed I am to have the chance to be the person I always wanted to be—a person you would have liked. I wish you had been able to be the person you wanted to be. I saw glimpses of her and she was a person I liked, loved, found funny, and admired.

If I had a chance to tell you, I would tell you that I forgive you and I love you.

Your daughter, Barbara

Accept Me Lovingly As Your Gay Daughter

I wish I didn't have to choose between my original family and my new one, but I'm an adult now. I've got to stop living my life to please you. I'll never fit the mold you set for me.

K.A.R., *Michigan*

Dear Mama,

I know you must be surprised to hear from me. I don't think I've ever written you a letter. I'd much rather talk to you in person, but we have trouble anytime a conversation drifts into certain areas of my life. We just say the same things over again, walking in verbal circles—tiptoeing and then stomping—each of us trying desperately to make her point and be understood.

This has been one of the best and, yes, one of the worst years of my life. In the last twelve months, I have finally found someone to share the rest of my life with, a soul mate, a partner. Regrettably, I have also watched my relationship with you disintegrate because of my new happiness. I have always known that you don't like the fact that I'm gay, but I guess I never realized the depth of your convictions. I had no idea you would actually choose your religious beliefs over your own flesh and blood. I never really believed it would get this bad between us . . . and we've had our fair share of bad times.

You've made your displeasure very clear. "I'd rather see you alone and miserable than happy with another woman." You aim for the jugular. Do you have any idea how badly it hurts to hear my own mother say something like that? Despite what you may feel, I need you to understand that Rose and I are in a committed relationship. We have pledged ourselves to one another—for better or worse, for richer or poorer, in sickness and in health. If we could make our union legal, we would.

I'd love to take her to North Carolina over the holidays to meet you and the family, to bring my two worlds together during this season of "brotherly love." But she's not welcome in your home. So much for the season of giving.

I wish I didn't have to choose between my original family and my new one, but I'm an adult now. I've got to stop living my life to please you. I'll never fit the mold you set for me.

It's time to stop apologizing for who I am. It's unfortunate that you feel my sexual orientation is "an abomination in the eyes of the Lord" because it keeps you from getting to know a truly remarkable woman—your own daughter. That little girl you gave birth to is now a grown woman full of deep thoughts and feelings, a woman whose character has been built on a foundation of honesty and integrity. You don't even know her. Her compassion for others and her capacity to love are matched only by her fierce loyalty to the people she cares about . . . and she cares about you.

Wednesday, November 13, 2002

You and I talked on the phone today. It's been awhile since our last conversation. You gave me an update on family news and talked about how holiday plans will be different this year now that Grandma has had to sell the house and move into a smaller place. You sounded sad. You said everyone was asking about me, that they were disappointed I wasn't going to join the festivities this year. I finally asked if you were giving a reason for my absence. I already knew the answer: "There isn't any need for people to know." I disagree, Ma. I'm tired of hiding "our dirty family secret" because you are ashamed of me.

When I realized you weren't going to change your mind about Rose coming with me, I decided to send Christmas cards to everyone. It's time to tell the truth. No ad in the paper. No billboard on the side of the road. A simple but clear message. A card "From the Two of Us" signed "Love, Kim and Rose."

I told you my plan. You hung up on me.

Monday, November 25, 2002

You called back a few days later. I was nervous about answering the phone. I never know what to expect. Well, that's not completely true. There is a pattern. You and I have a disagreement, we go off to deal with our pain, and then you call me back and act as if nothing has happened. True to form, you never mentioned Thanksgiving, even though it's only three days away. You never asked about my plans; you didn't tell me yours. It was a superficial conversation, but I enjoyed it nonetheless. Despite what you may think, I miss you.

Wednesday, November 27, 2002

When you called at 10:00 a.m. and left a message, I got a hollow, sick feeling in my stomach, wondering what your message would say. It's the day before Thanksgiving, and we've both held our ground. For the first time ever, I'm not flying to North Carolina for this holiday. It feels weird and I'm sad. I type in an effort to keep from crying.

I never imagined it would come to this; I guess I'm just too naïve. I actually thought that you and Daddy would eventually change your minds and let me bring Rose home to meet the family. Not a whole weekend. Just a few hours. I really believed that you would want to see me badly enough to compromise. It blows my mind.

The holidays have always been special to me, but for a different reason than for you. My holidays are about family. All family—old and new. You know that I don't share your beliefs regarding the religious significance of Christmas. I don't understand your Baptist God—the God that you say is going to send me to hell for my sin of homosexuality. You don't seem to understand that God made me this way. We must agree to disagree on this one. I know he created me in his own image and loves me just as I am. Let's stop fighting about this. PLEASE.

I've given up hope for your acceptance. Now I'm fearful that even tolerance is out of reach.

I'm going to go call you now. I wonder what you'll have to say. I never know what to expect. Oh, yeah, I forgot. We do have that pattern. They say that insanity is

doing the same thing over again and expecting different re
sults. I don't know what else to say, Mama. I don't want to
go crazy.

I love you.

K.A.R.

Accepting My Body and Loving Myself

I still feel so helpless, frustrated, and hurt because I desired so deeply to know you loved me, not just the perfect little girl I attempted to be.

ANNA CLINE, *Pennsylvania*

Dear Mama,

Is there any longing deeper than the desire for connection from child to mother? If there is, perhaps it's the simultaneous pull to separate into a distinct individual. For years, I have longed to bond to you through love and intimacy. Instead, I bonded with your pain and took it as mine to bear. My years-long struggle with anorexia nervosa chronicles my attempt to pull free and separate what is me from what is you.

Mama, I have never wanted to hurt you. I need to tell you first that I love you. I long to get past the emotional shield you hold up and know you as a mother and a person.

I long to be known and heard and loved by you. I haven't known where I stood with you. Was I in the way? Did you hate me? I never knew if I was acceptable or not. I still feel so helpless, frustrated, and hurt because I desired so deeply to know you loved me, not just the perfect little girl I attempted to be. Maybe if I tried hard enough, I could please you and make you happy. Then you would really love me! I hid myself behind a smiling mask of perfection because the real me was blackened by the shame of sadness and anger that wasn't supposed to exist.

Part of my eating disorder has been about getting rid of the shame of who I am—getting rid of me. The real me didn't seem good enough, no matter how hard I tried. Did you see me, Mama? Did you see how hard I tried?

I am so tired of trying, and I am angry that I had to sacrifice myself to be accepted. I am angry that you weren't there for me. Yes, physically you were with me, yet I could never really reach you. I am so confused. Who should I be to merit your love? My soul cries out because I only want a mother and I want her to be you. I may be a mother now, but I still need one!

I felt so responsible for you, Mama. Though I was the child, I thought I should be the one protecting you. You showed me a distant, cold exterior, and yet I sensed the depth of your own pain. No one ever talked about it, including me. I wanted to reach you behind your walls. I wanted my love for you to be enough to heal you. I now know that no child can heal a mother's pain. I didn't know that when I was only a small girl. Since I couldn't make you whole, I tried to take the brokenness away. Little by little, I absorbed it until your suffering became mine and fused into my longing for a mother's love.

I have become your mirror, Mama. I didn't ask for this job, but I took it on me. You've watched me these last twelve years as I've modeled the family pain. I've been performing a slow dance of death with anorexia. I saw tears in your eyes for the first time whenever you heard me talk about why I need to wither away. Those tears watered the garden of my hope, not just for me, but for you, too. Did you know that you weren't just crying for me, but for yourself?

Anorexia strips away the denial of our grief. I am tired of masks and pretension. I can't pretend that it didn't hurt when there was time for all the others except me, when my childhood tears dried alone, when my longing to be held and loved remained empty. It is your loss, too! I am angry that I am the one with the problem now. The family fingers all point at me. Please look past your pretending and see what I am saying!

I see past the mask when I look at you. Past the anger, past the hurt and fear, past a lifetime of deep grief lies a little girl who grew into a woman's body with more little girls to raise. I see that child-woman who made the best choices she could at the time.

Mama, I offer forgiveness to you, and I reach out to ask

you to join me on this journey of healing. I want to be who I was created to be now, and I won't take responsibility for you anymore. I hope you will like who I have become. I am working hard to heal, but I want that for you, too. You may not have an eating disorder that is physically destroying you, but deep inside, you need rebuilding.

Let me in. Let others in. I want to love you and I want you to feel it. Like you, I have huge walls around me. I am choosing to tear them down, brick by brick. You can choose the same. I will not stop or turn back, but my heart longs to have you here with me. I have my own little girl now and I must find a way to stop the tradition of hurt and hiding.

Love,

Your oldest daughter, Anna

Freedom from Anger

*As I revised my letter, I found myself slipping into my
mother's shoes. I began to identify with the humiliation
and lack of power she must feel now that she's less independent. My anger gradually changed to compassion.*
ANNE WARREN SMITH, *Oregon*

A few years after my mother recovered, we were traveling
together for the first time as adults to Los Angeles for
my sister's wedding shower. Because we were excited about
the moments we'd spend together and with my sister, taking
this trip sounded and felt wonderful. Yet our vision for the
weekend didn't exactly match what transpired.

My mother, who was having a difficult time hormonally,
found it challenging to travel five hours on a plane. The seat-
ing arrangements and loud noises aggravated her. At night in

our hotel room, when I wanted to sleep, she couldn't rest, resulting in sleep deprivation. She'd suddenly switch on the lights and wake me up. After a series of such moments, our anger toward each other intensified.

On our trip back to Miami, our flight got canceled in Atlanta. We waited long hours at the airport before being transferred to another flight. Our surly glances toward one another intensified. By this time, our voices were filled with frustration and impatience. On our return flight into Miami, we decided to sit apart and not speak to each other. After landing, my mother stormed ahead of me and said I was a good daughter from afar, but not close up. Our anger got the best of both us. We stomped off in opposite directions.

I felt virtuous when I thought about my side of this story with my mother, yet I also felt unsettled and saddened by our argument. Awakened again to the memory of her almost dying four years before, that aching voice inside my heart cried out, "At any moment, your mother could be gone. The meaning of life is far beyond right, wrong, or ego. It's love that matters the most." As many of the wise masters remind us, mindful practices in our everyday lives guide us to what's most precious in the moment.

When I went over these thoughts in my head, my irritations subsided instantaneously. The next day, I sent Mom a note saying, "We may not always agree on ‿ut I will always love you with all my heart."

Most of us have weathered storms like this many times before. Powerful emotions are triggered and both end up in a frenzy with smoke coming out our ears. Our anger temporarily or sometimes permanently blinds us from the love we feel for each other. We expect the moon, then feel offended when the picture doesn't end up as we envisioned, as on this trip with my mother.

Sometimes our mothers hurt us tremendously, and we can't seem to shake off the bad feelings. One minute, we're enjoying a grand day; the next minute, they say something that spurs a deeply held hurt from long ago. In these sudden outbursts, we're ready to point the finger at everyone around us. Recycling the unresolved anger that festers within turns into a dangerous explosion.

For some of the writers in this chapter, it would have been easier to blame their mothers forever for what they endured in their childhood. They demonstrate that a seed of fury can manifest into our own worst enemy. Yet they also teach us that anger can strengthen us if acknowledged and dealt with.

As these daughters write to their mothers, their anger transforms into compassion and understanding. Some letters show us that although we can love our mothers unconditionally, it's still vitally important to accept our anger toward them as a part of the integral self, as part of growth. As Anne Warren Smith wrote, "When a friend read an early draft of my letter, she pointed out my anger—anger that was there because of the way my mother often reduced me to a child. I was surprised at the depth of my anger. As I revised my letter, I found myself slipping into my mother's shoes. I began to identify with the humiliation and lack of power she must feel now that she's less independent. My anger gradually changed to compassion."

Life can be fleeting if we dwell in a destructive rage. The golden key is to move beyond the fire as anger surfaces and nurture it through supportive practices every day. Over time, the anger arises but dissipates quickly. It is important to embrace anger as a transformative and resourceful emotion—seeing what it can teach us about ourselves.

Why Did You Ignore Your Health?

You ignored the very large and obvious lump in your armpit for years. I have chosen not to dwell on what could have been if you would have faced the cancer immediately.

JESSICA (JETTE) STEPHENS, *California*

Dear Mom,

I am writing you this to let you know how much I love you and to thank you for being the best mother I could ever ask for. You are my hero. Everything about you amazes me, and I admire your ability to love your family. I admire your success, positive attitude, kindness, generosity, bravery, determination, and can-do-anything attitude. You have always loved me unconditionally, giving me wonderful childhood memories and an education. You believed in me when everyone else doubted me (especially myself). You never judged me and didn't stop me from doing things even if you may not have agreed with them. Thank you for saving me during my teenage years when everybody gave up on me. Thank you for encouraging me to succeed and be happy. You truly have made me a better person, and I am honored to be your daughter.

I have all this love and appreciation for you, and that is why I feel so angry. I am angry because you are leaving this world and I am not ready for you to go. It isn't fair what is happening to our family. You are dying at a young age, and I feel guilty for thinking this, but it's kind of your fault. You ignored the very large and obvious lump in your armpit for years. How could you deny it when breast cancer awareness is always in your face? Did you forget that your mother had it, too? I know we reminded you to get mammograms. Didn't you go? You are the most intelligent person I have ever known. I don't understand why you were in such denial. Was it because you didn't have time to be sick? Was it because having cancer would interfere with your career? Well, now look! Your denial is costing you your life and every member of our family is being cheated out of a future with you in it.

I am angry because every day for the rest of my life I will feel empty because I won't be able to see you or hear your voice when I tell you good news. I won't be able to cry on your shoulder when something goes wrong or take your advice when I don't know what to do. You won't be here for the birth of my future children or to watch them grow up. You won't see me as a mother or watch me live out my dreams. I am going to miss you so much, and I hate looking into my future without you in it.

Although it frustrates me that you pretended nothing was wrong with you, I do forgive you for the denial you were in. I am able to forgive you because I know you didn't mean any of this to happen. Even when the lump got so big that you couldn't put your arm all the way down, I know that you never imagined it would come to this point. I can forgive you because I have learned so many things from watching you battle cancer.

I have become a stronger person as a result of your illness. I have learned to take care of myself and not ignore my body. I watched as cancer took everything away from you—your hair, your breasts, your comfort, your mind, your dignity, and now your life. I admire you for finally facing this disease and hitting it head-on as hard as you could while maintaining a positive attitude the entire time. With all of the strength and integrity you put into the fight, how could I not forgive you?

Before you leave this world, I want to promise you that I will move forward and I will succeed in life. It is your belief in me that will keep me going after you're gone.

As my mother, I want you to do two more things for me. First, I want you to forgive yourself as I have forgiven you. There is no reason to mentally beat yourself up anymore.

Secondly, I want you to let go and end this suffering. You don't have to hold on for our family any longer. You and Dad love each other and have raised three children who grew up to be commendable adults. Let go, knowing that you were a successful mother. We're going to feel sad, and it's going to hurt when we lose you. But because of you, eventually we will be ok.

Even though you won't be by my side, I promise that you will be in my heart forever, and I will take you with me everywhere I go.

I will always love you, Jette

The Secret Ingredients of Spaghetti Sauce

Although our worlds are different now, our spirits are still here. They whisper, "Believe in God, Believe in yourself."
PATRICIA HUBER, *California*

Dear Mother,

As I stand here stirring the spaghetti, I think of you with happy thoughts. Such a revelation since so many of them have been sad or angry. I realize now that it was your secret ingredients that made the spaghetti so delicious. Even when you felt ill, you always made sure I had my favorite spaghetti casserole the second day.

There were good times before I turned thirteen and you turned to alcohol. I was a free spirit. Roller-skating in the wind with it to push me rather than pushing against it. Playing house and being a royal princess. Or maybe I was the wicked witch. Being a witch wasn't so bad because it gave me control over something. Others ran from me in fear. I wasn't the runner.

Magic was with me then. You let us set up a tent on the side of the house where I could play fortune-teller. My upside-down fishbowl predicted marvelous things. You smiled when I divined that you'd make your pot roast and mashed potatoes.

I think you believed in the magic. You told me stories of fairies and leprechauns. I'd find you reading a book when I came home from school. Naturally, I wanted to read one, too. Thank you for the forever love of books. They were and are magic.

You also quoted poetry. In times when life gets tedious, I find myself taking out Walt Whitman or Yeats. They tell me it isn't tedious at all but a wonderful story, writing itself every second, finding its nourishment from a peaceful brook or star-sparkled evening. Thank you for my poetry worlds.

But soon the drinking came to claim your world—the screaming at me through the bathroom door that I'd never amount to anything. You were screaming at yourself, weren't you, Mother, trying to yell away your demons? What pain you must have been in. The liquor only temporarily dulled the thoughts, just to trick you. Like Alice in Wonderland, you tried the "Drink Me" bottle, which distorted your realness.

Mother, I understand it now. I've felt the same need to have that drink after a terrible day. I've had the same hangover. But fear of facing *your* hell has stopped me from doing it very often. I'm one of the lucky ones. I can enjoy a drink and not let the drink enjoy me.

In a strange way, you taught me to turn to a better panacea. I've learned how to meditate. I turn to God and let my thoughts stay on my mantra: *Your love, Lord.* Mentally, I repeat it until I fall into a deep peace. Questions that plagued me are answered. There's no need to dial the 911 of emotional distress. He's there seeing beyond my pain, helping me know that I'm not a bad girl—only a loved girl.

"I'm sorry, Pat," you've said. "Please forgive me. I've always loved you. I was wrong to call you a bad girl. You are a great woman. How could I ever say a thing like that? Mine was a great unhappiness. The only good part of my life was you."

Mom, I have even cried for you. I'll try to forgive you even if it takes all of my life. Forgiveness comes like a tiny brook ripple until it makes its way to release in the ocean. I don't begrudge your happiness. You've had enough ugliness in your life.

A friend helped me see the other side through meditation. First, he asked me to tell him all the things about you that were hurtful. I made a list: my crying, how you weren't there, how you screamed that I was terrible, your falling down drunk and insisting on remaining on the floor helplessly, telling me not to get angry or you'd call the police, and telling me not to act silly. I took each memory and they became ashes. I swept them away with my broom. Then it was time to transform the ashes—to rise like a phoenix. I dreamt about the new, true mother who did the opposite of what I experienced. The mother who cradled me when I cried. The mother who held me close and told me it was all right. The mother who didn't scream obscenities. She merely told me what she'd like to see me do without any anger in her voice. She didn't fall drunk for she had no need to drink. If I got angry, the new mother would let me express my anger so I could move on. If I wanted to be silly, why not?

I see the true you, Mother. Let's forget the sadness and walk a new walk together. We'll get angry, we'll get silly, we'll live.

Although our worlds are different now, our spirits are still here. They whisper, "Believe in God. Believe in yourself."

It is time, Mother. I know you believed in God with your work on the Altar Guild. Now believe in the brilliant, talented, lovely woman who was always within you. I'm so glad to meet you.

Love, Patricia

After Thirty Years, How Could You?

Please understand, Mommy, I'm not your friend, and I'm not your doctor. I am your daughter, and I deserve peace.

TAMMY GARTLEY, *Illinois*

Dear Momma,
Divorce; how could you?

I cried last night. I cried until my eyes were red and my face swollen. I cannot do this any longer. I am not a therapist, and I'm not a marriage counselor. This is harder on me than anything I could ever imagine. You've been together for thirty years. I can't come to grips with you and Daddy getting divorced now. What will you do? Where will he live? Where will we go on holidays? Do you have someone else? Does he? What will my friends say? Dammit! Mom, why now, after thirty years?

Yeah, I know. I grew up knowing all I wasn't supposed to know. I know he's not a great lover. I know he drinks way too much. I know he never takes you anywhere. But *thirty years*? I can't cope with this, and I refuse to let you and him stress me.

Please understand, Mommy, I'm not your friend, and I'm not your doctor. I am your daughter, and I deserve peace. I am walking away from this situation. When I see you again, I want to know how your day went, not how he's treating you, or mistreating you. I want to know how the sun shone your way today. I don't want to hear about how he doesn't talk to you anymore, how he doesn't love you anymore.

I want to be invisible in all of this. I want to be a kid, even though I'm an adult. I want to be silent. I want to be your daughter again.

So now I'm leaving all this behind. When I walk into the house tomorrow, I want to see you smile and ask me about my day. I want to smell cornbread cooking and see you fixing my plate. I want my life back, no matter how superficial or fake it is. I want to be your baby girl.

I love you, Mommy. Do you love me? Yes or no.

Tammy

Relying on Myself

Ultimately, your mental illness taught me to rely on myself. I had to grow up from one day to the next. I learned that no one is invulnerable to life's difficulties.

ISABEL SANCHEZ, *Florida*

Dear Mami,

There are so many things I want to tell you. How much I love you, admire you, and look up to you. Through your inspiration, I've learned to be independent and strong, but beautiful and feminine at the same time—a delicate balance to maintain.

It's always been you and me against the world. For most of my life, you've been the center of my universe, the prism through which I viewed my life. You were always sturdy as a rock, my support. I knew I could rely on you to fix any problem. You always had the answer.

Until the day you got sick. That's when my world changed forever. You were no longer sturdy, strong, and independent. Suddenly you became helpless, dependent, and fearful of everything around you.

At first, I didn't even know you were sick. You believed people were after us, trying to kill us by poisoning our food, planting microphones all over the house to listen to our conversations, and following me on school field trips. I also believed these things were happening. Whatever you said was always the right thing. Because you were the prism I viewed my life through, the world around me was distorted. I became paranoid along with you, suspicious of everyone and everything. I couldn't imagine that you were a paranoid schizophrenic.

When your best friend and my godmother finally convinced you to go to the doctor and you were diagnosed, my whole world fell apart. I would much rather have lived in a world where people were trying to kill us than one in which my mother was crazy.

Before you got sick, you and I had an amazing relationship. We talked for hours like two best friends, and I never felt the need to keep any secrets from you. I had the freedom to do whatever I wanted and go wherever I wanted. My house was the official sleepover site for all of my girlfriends. But all of that changed.

During your disease, you couldn't take care of yourself, much less your fourteen-year-old daughter. So I became the mother. Every morning before school, I'd make sure you took your medicine and had some breakfast. I'd spend the day at school worrying about you, wondering if you would try to kill yourself again, or if I would come home to find all of the wires in the house cut because you thought they were cables for microphones and tiny cameras used by people to spy on us. I made you something to eat, gave you your medicines again, and tried to do my homework. I didn't go out with my friends because I was afraid to leave you alone. I never had friends over because I was too ashamed of my crazy mother.

Those two years of your disease were the most terrifying of my life. It pained me to see how you had deteriorated. Before your illness, your beauty caused heads to turn as you walked down the street. Your long, blond hair framed your pale face and complemented your blue eyes. You were tall, svelte, and statuesque. Women and men alike commented on your beauty. But during your illness, your beauty withered. Your hair thinned and became brittle, your eyes dimmed, your skin became dry and flaky, and you got so thin and frail, I feared you'd break in half if I hugged you too hard.

While I was taking care of you, I was scared and angry with you for getting sick. I felt cheated of a normal adolescence. I was angry at my father for not being there for us, for forcing me to be the one to take responsibility. I felt so alone because I was too ashamed to tell my friends about what I was going through. I wanted to blame you for everything that was happening, but I knew it wasn't your fault.

Ultimately, your sickness taught me to rely on myself. I had to grow up from one day to the next. I learned that no one is invulnerable to life's difficulties. You have to be ready for everything. Most important, I learned that anything could be overcome. No matter how hopeless a situation seems, it will end and life will go on.

Thankfully, you got better. Your illness has never entirely gone away, but you're able to live on your own. I know your disease will always haunt us, and it will probably pop up again, but I know we can deal with it, together.

I love you,

Your daughter Helen

An Outsider in My Own Home

I have been trying to escape the feeling of not being good enough for as long as I can remember.
COURTNEA W. SMITH STARK, *New York*

Dear Mommy,

I have decided to write you, even though you will not respond in the conventional way.

The night that you died, I was so stunned. I was sleeping next to you, and I awoke to what I thought was you snoring, but actually you were dying. I felt cold, scared, lonely, left— all at the same time.

I am somehow sure you must know, your sister Marion took Stanley and I into her house. I often wonder if you were watching over me during those three years. Were you angry about the way I was treated?

Did you know I was to become a slave to them? Did you know I wore the same pair of shoes (the ones you bought me the summer before you left) for three years? Did you know their only interest in me was to be able to purchase our house and make it theirs, forcing me to be an outsider in my own home?

I have been trying to escape the feeling of not being good enough for as long as I can remember.

It hurt not to have you there when I graduated high school, when I got married, and when my children were born.

For many years, I was rebellious and angry. I felt that rebellion was one way of shielding me, by not showing how hurt I was. I did not recognize the anger until many years later. Then I was angry over everything—the weather, the job, the kids, the relationships. Everything made me mad as hell.

This anger has taken its toll on me in many ways, most particularly my health.

Even now I must accomplish something every day, and I feel guilty if I don't. Perhaps this "work ethic" was a gift from you. I remember that you were always working hard, trying to give us food and shelter.

Perhaps because I didn't have a mommy for much of my life, I have made it a point to be there for my two children. By the way, I named my only daughter after you. Her middle name is Helen, so in a way you are still here and very much a part of my day-to-day thinking.

I wonder how we would see each other now, since I am fifty-seven and you would be ninety-two. I am a believer. I look forward to our meeting again one day. I am sure we will have lots to talk about and lots of lost time to make up for. There were many times I couldn't have cared less whether we met again or not. But I do care now.

It's hard for me to write this letter since I barely knew you when you left. I wondered for years what you were thinking of me, and if I entered your thoughts ever.

My biggest regret is that I never knew much of your life history, and so I can't really tell your grandchildren about you.

My wish for you now is that you are at peace and have no regrets about your short time here on earth.

Still missing you.

With love,

Your daughter

No Le Pidas Peras al Olmo
(Don't Ask an Elm Tree for Pears)

*For most of my life I've been asking and expecting you to
give me what you didn't have and couldn't give.*
MARISOL MUÑOZ KIEHNE, PH.D., *California*

Dear Mami,
Lately I've been thinking about mothers. More than about
mothers in general, about you, my mother, and about *abuela,*
your mother. I've been recalling all sorts of memories from
our past. Remember *abuela*'s Puerto Rican sayings? I'm
writing this letter to share with you some of what I am learning about mothers from one of those sayings, the one telling
us not to expect pears from elm trees.

When I first heard this saying a long time ago, I didn't understand its meaning or recognize its wisdom. It seemed obvious to me that elm trees would not produce pears. Yet, it is
now that I'm almost forty years old, and after living through
struggle and grief, that this old saying is beginning to make

sense to me. More than comprehending its significance, I am feeling its power, and it is guiding me closer to you. You see, Mami, you are like an elm tree—or more like a pine tree—and for most of my life I've been asking and expecting you to give me what you didn't have and couldn't give.

As a young girl, I wanted a funny, playful, joyful mother, which you were not. I used to compare you with some of my friends' mothers, who were as colorful as maple trees in autumn. I rejoiced in the fascinating hues of their leaves, which turned yellow, orange, red, even purple! And I turned green with envy watching other kids jump on piles of crisp maple leaves. I wished I could have fun like that at home. I waited for my pine tree to change, to be more like a maple tree. I asked my pine tree for colorful leaves that would later fall into crunchy heaps.

And I waited . . . patiently for a while, then impatiently. Mami, you were the serious, monochromatic, quiet type of mother who didn't laugh out loud or frolic with abandon. Working and worrying were more familiar to you than fun and games.

I also longed for a mother like those I read about in children's books. Those mothers were like oak trees, with massive, sturdy branches good for climbing. I had a great time climbing up oak trees in my imagination, going from branch to branch, until reaching a high point from where I could see far away in the distance. But my pine tree didn't have branches I could climb.

Angry, I used to curse, punch, and kick my pine tree. But as much as I threatened and fought with my tree, it still didn't grow branches I could climb. Mami, your arms and hands were fragile, you seemed tired all the time, and were often sick. I felt frustrated, mad, enraged at times, and afraid that my anger would hurt you. I felt cheated. It wasn't fair. I wanted a healthy, strong mother on whose shoulders I could climb on to glean a future full of vitality in the distance,

As a teenager I fantasized about my mother being like my favorite movie stars, who, like magnolia trees, had fragrant, exotic blossoms that illuminated their surroundings with their presence. I was enthralled by the beauty and scent of the flowers, and pretended to put them on my hair, pin them on my dresses, and design romantic bouquets.

Coming home to my pine tree, I bargained for it to produce flowers. But no amount of bargaining, pleading, or daring would bring about the desired result. My pine tree kept generating a pine scent, not flowers or a floral scent. Mami, you were not the beautiful mother whose genes would make me a beautiful woman. Your scent was not erotic and irresistible; it was clean and sanitized. I wanted an attractive, sexy model from whom to learn about beauty secrets and sensual pleasures. And I wanted to find in my mother a mirror for the bright light I sensed from my soul. But you could not be that model or that mirror. You didn't know your own beauty or your own light.

All this time I was also hungry. Ravenous for warm hugs and a mom's homemade pie. I craved the delicious, nutritious fruit I saw or imagined hanging from mother trees all around me. Like those sweet, juicy, luscious pears that seemed to grow everywhere except at home.

Mami, you couldn't satisfy my hunger, for you yourself hadn't been nurtured. Little orphan *abuela* didn't have a mother to feed her, and grew up like Cinderella with an evil stepmother. So, you were famished, not having been hugged and loved as a little girl. Your breast was dry. Your heart was hiding. You couldn't fall in love with me, your daughter, or allow me to need you, to attach to you, and to love you, because you didn't know how, and were afraid. You couldn't meet my needs for attention and affection. I believe that's one reason why my eyes seem sad in many of my childhood photos.

But, Mami, my eyes are not sad anymore. Our story didn't end there. I was feeling very unhappy, sobbing by my pine tree, when it happened. Something wet had plopped on my left shoe. Looking up, I saw a bird in a nest, perched right over my head. I noticed that the nest was made out of leaves from maple trees, twigs from oak trees, and old flowers from magnolia trees, as well as needles from pine trees.

That's when I experienced an important insight. I got it! I had failed to make my pine tree give me what it could not give me. I did not want to believe that it would never have colorful leaves, so I kept asking. I got angry at my pine tree for not having climbing branches. I bargained for flowers, and cried over not having fruit. Still my pine tree had remained a pine tree, and I was miserable. That's when I decided to do like the bird did in building its nest, and look for what I need or want in the places where I may find it.

Mami, I am sorry that, for a long time, we both struggled with ourselves and with each other, standing close enough to hurt, but not to embrace each other. I regret the harsh words I used toward you, and the harsher silences and walls I erected between us. I regret the time gone and the opportunities wasted. I apologize for my stubbornness. And I grieve. I grieve for myself, for you, and for *abuela*, three generations of daughters who craved pears and were raised by pine trees.

Little by little, I am coming to terms with it all. I am learning to accept my pine tree as a pine tree. I go to maple trees when wanting to jump on piles of leaves, to oak trees when I feel like climbing up high to see far away, to magnolia trees when in the mood for flowers, and to pear trees when hungry for fruit.

Even better, I now feel sincere gratitude for what you were and are able to offer me. I see in the way you've lived your life admirable examples of endurance, persistence, industriousness, humility, integrity, faith, and much more. Mami, I am coming to appreciate my pine tree's virtues. No piles of colorful leaves, but a cool shade all year long. No climbing branches, but fine pine needles to make garlands and wreaths. No aromatic flowers, but fresh pine fragrance. No sweet pears, but woody pinecones.

Mami, you know what? Looking back and looking at myself now, I'd say my pine tree gave me much more than enough to grow on. My eyes sparkle now, for I'm no longer sad, and I don't go hungry anymore.

Still growing under your shade,

Your daughter

Goodbye to Guilt

I felt unworthy and guilty for abandoning my mother on her deathbed. I was angry and punishing myself. The guilt festered for years, and I became jaded, hostile, and bitter. I realized that emotions are the core of the soul, and that to deny your feelings is to deny yourself.

LYN DANO, *Georgia*

As a woman, I often feel as if the word *guilt* is branded on my forehead. Sometimes I think it's an absolute miracle that I have experienced even one joyous moment, given all the confusing cultural messages passed on to us. How can we possibly find our way back to innocence when we feel so guilty about everything, even about not feeling bad enough?

Joan Borysenko, Ph.D., author of *Guilt Is the Teacher, Love Is the Lesson,* challenges us to rise above our everyday thinking. "We are each a composite, a mosaic of different thoughts, emotions, and choices of behavior. Each of us is more mature in some areas than in others. This doesn't make us 'bad'—it just means that we have certain 'growing edges.' Rather than thinking in terms of good and bad, it is more helpful to think in terms of conscious and unconscious, aware and unaware."

Examining guilt in these terms, I'm reminded of two women, unrelated and from different backgrounds, whose stories best depict the differences between holding on to unnecessary guilt and letting it go.

Born into a wealthy family, Lynn had always been given whatever she wanted. As a teenager, she "escaped" by getting heavily involved in drugs to the point of smashing several brand-new cars, getting thrown in jail, and struggling to stay alive. She put her parents and her entire family through severe emotional turmoil for years.

Lynn went into therapy and joined Alcoholics Anonymous. She recovered from her alcoholism completely and has been living a healthy life for more than ten years. Unfortunately, both her parents passed away before seeing her transformation, and she continues to chastise herself for how she treated her parents in the past. Lynn is haunted by her wish to turn back the clock.

Rachel dealt with her guilt in a very different way. She became a mother at a young age and also an alcoholic. She hardly knew how to take care of herself, let alone her children. She was seen as unfit by many in the family, and her children were taken away to live with their grandparents. As Rachel matured and went into recovery, she realized what a terrible mistake she had made. She literally woke up from a drunken stupor. As she did, her guilt burdened and terrified her. Gradually, through working hard to change herself, she was able to make amends with all of her children and live a somewhat healthy life. Rachel came to a place of peace before she passed away.

Guilt is a hefty emotion to deal with if, like Lynn, we constantly doubt our own judgments and those of others. By never letting go of the blunders of yesterday, we remain stuck in a world that perpetuates our pain, and we can't feel justified in moving on. On the other hand, like Rachel, we also have the option of viewing guilt from a new perspective, of "growing our edges."

Throughout the letters in this chapter, women bring to light the struggles associated with guilt. They call out to our own haunted desires that tempt us to stray from being our very best. We have lived our dilemmas of whether we could have done more to help. We're concerned about the promises we never kept, the decisions we wish we could have changed, the lack of unconditional care for our loved ones, and the pain of unresolved feelings.

We can't erase our agonizing mistakes, yet we all deserve to forgive ourselves and begin again. If we concentrate on making things better in the moment, we can be eternally grateful for another opportunity to live our lives in healthier, more fulfilling ways.

The women in this book inspire us to continue forward without feeling guilty about the past. As poet Maya Angelou says, "You did what you knew how to do, and when you knew better, you did better." In the heart and soul of life, this is really all that matters.

My Heart-Wrenching Decision

Any tiny doubts that may have been lurking within me have been released because the doctor reaffirmed that my decision to operate was the best decision I have ever made.

JUDY BRAND, *Texas*

Dear, dear Mother,
Together we will read this letter. I am writing it for us to share. If I deliver it at a time when you think I am your sister, I will save it for a better day—a day when you remember that I am your daughter.

Don't worry, I will read slowly and watch for a spark of understanding in your eyes. If your pupils begin to dart around the room and your good hand starts to crinkle your bedsheet, I will stop reading. We will wait and continue on a better day.

Finally, when that day comes, I will tell you about that depression in your forehead. You know, that hole in your skull that spreads confusion over your face when you rub it.

Almost twenty years ago, there was an explosion in your head while you were giving a speech. That indentation was drilled as an entrance to your brain. A neurosurgeon threaded the damaged area together so that your life could continue.

That is my fault. I am the one who begged him to save you when he gave me a choice. I thought that life, any life, was better than death. I was unaware that you would be entirely dependent on others for survival or that you would never again have one moment of privacy or that you would fabricate a new identity for yourself and all of us. I was selfish, without realizing it, when I refused to let go of your life.

After your surgery, I silently questioned my decision to keep you alive in a state of diminished dignity. At the time of your operation, the surgeon also questioned the decision.

For a short time, friends came to visit you in the nursing home. When you didn't recognize them or you spoke irrationally, their visits ceased. Fortunately, you didn't seem to notice.

"She would never have wanted to be like this," they said, hurrying away as though your situation might be contagious. They overlooked your happiness and smiles, focusing only on a person they no longer understood.

For me, your happiness and smiles mask the confusion that plays hide-and-seek in your brain. You, my new mother, have brought joy to my family and me.

My children have enjoyed more years with you since the aneurysm than they shared with you before. The three of you never made that trip to Las Vegas that you planned. The children still haven't. For years, they hoped you would have a miraculous recovery and be well enough to accompany them.

I wonder if you realize that you have six little great-granddaughters. When you met the first one, she named you Grandmother Great. When they come in from Kansas, you are the first person they want to visit. You don't seem to mind when they pull cookies from your food tray. Did you know you're the only great-grandparent they have?

With you, we have celebrated twenty years of holidays and birthdays in this nursing home. You've been here longer than any other resident and you thrive in this surreal environment.

Yesterday, at a lecture, I saw the neurosurgeon who operated on you. He was on the opposite side of a crowded room. When the lecture was about to begin, I pointed him out to Kelly, my daughter. You remember Kelly, right? She was here yesterday to visit. Kelly was so excited that she hurried across the room to talk to the doctor, then made it back as the speaker approached the podium.

When I looked for the doctor at the end of the lecture, he had melded into the crowd. Then Kelly excitedly shared the details of her conversation with him. When she told him that he had operated on her grandmother, his eyes lit up. He remembered you and the complex operation that kept you alive.

He told Kelly that he'd always wondered if he had done the right thing in performing an operation on a brain so severely damaged. He had two questions for Kelly. He wanted to know if you had the ability to enjoy life and he wanted to know if we enjoyed *you*. She said that you'd lived twenty happy years since the surgery. Then she told him that one of the most important things in her life was having a grandmother to love during those years.

He smiled at her and said, "Then it was the correct decision to operate."

Mother, if you are confused by this letter, don't worry. I had to share this news even if you don't understand it. Any tiny doubts that may have been lurking within me have been released because the doctor reaffirmed that my decision to operate was the best decision I have ever made.

Continue to smile and be happy, dear Mother.

Your loving daughter, Judy

Release This Guilt

The carrying of this guilt has made me feel unworthy and undeserving of love.

LYN DANO, *Georgia*

Dearest Mom,

During the days before you died, I felt you were hanging on because you were waiting for me to say good-bye. I'm *so* sorry for not being there when you were dying. We shared so many wonderful memories, and for selfish reasons, I didn't want my last memory to be of your death. I didn't want to be haunted by that image. I placed distance between us to block the pain, which was enormous. I was so confused and angry that you were dying because of your drinking. I was hurt and powerless because I felt you were committing a slow suicide. I felt guilty because I thought maybe there was more I could have done to stop it. I was depressed and helpless because I kept wondering what was so bad and painful in your life that you would choose to drown in alcohol. Alcohol became an obstacle and barrier causing distance between us.

The only thing that made sense to me at the time was to run. I can only imagine the pain and fear you must have felt. You must have felt alone and abandoned. But, Mom, please understand it was because I loved you so much that I couldn't be there to watch you die. I'm asking you to please forgive me. I need your forgiveness so I can release my guilt and move on with my life. The carrying of this guilt has made me feel unworthy and undeserving of love. In turn, I'm filled with rage and hostility, becoming cold and callous as well as unwilling to give love.

That is *not* how you were, Mom. You were the source of love. From you, I learned the meaning of unconditional love. I want to be able to feel love again and to share it because *I know* that's what you would want for me to do.

So please, help me to release this guilt. I am not saying good-bye to you or your memories—just to the guilt—so I can have my soul back. Please stay with me as I walk through the rest of my life, doing and being the best I can because that's what you'd expect from me.

Forever you are always in all ways, Mom, Lyn

True Home Is Far Away

You have been "home" for me for so many years.
JOSETTE WALLACE, *Hawaii*

Dear Mommy,

I remember sitting on the hillside, looking over a loch with the heather all around, though it was past its best bloom. The world was bright and beautiful, and we sat there together, although it was cold, and we were happy. Weren't we? I sometimes wonder if the past is only so happy in memory, or if it's just happier than the uncertain future that approaches.

I have only begun to look back into my past and find things that I think of as big regrets. There have always been oopses, questionable incidents, even a few small glitches, but only now am I finding, in my personal journal of memories, what I call big mistakes.

And I can't name them.

I remember Daddy saying that the best part of traveling is coming home. I think, at first blush, that the best part of traveling is leaving, and then I change and think, no, it *is* coming home. And then I realize the best part of traveling is when you can, and do, and will distill what is "home" into the most essential things that you need. You take those essentials with you.

You have been "home" for me for so many years now. It doesn't matter where you are; you are home. Which is why, when we traveled together, I was never sorry to leave "home," never needed to get "home," because "home"—true Home—was with me. True Home placed a cool hand on my forehead one morning in Scotland when we were afraid I was getting sick. True Home held me when I cried over the little things and the big things. True Home fought with me, angered me, and loved me just the same all the time. I knew that Home would love me forever.

And now Home is far away from me, and I'm terrified that Home will get farther away from me soon—that I may never be able to be Home again. And I don't know what to do.

But one thing I can do is clear up some of the small mistakes, even if I can't take away the big ones. Something has been bugging me so much lately. When I cook a meal and hope that someone will like it, I think of something that happened—you had made a goulash kind of meal once. It had beans, meat, and noodles, and I didn't want to eat it. I said it looked like—well, you actually finished the sentence, and you were mad and very upset. I remember thinking that if you just cooked stuff I liked, we wouldn't have this problem. I didn't understand then what it was like to put a meal together out of nothing, to experiment and be pleased with the result, and to have no one like it with you. That was a small mistake, and I'm sorry. I just wanted to tell you that.

I am afraid now of doing things I wish I could take back, make right, and apologize so they will go away. But the essence of big mistakes, as opposed to small ones, is that "I'm sorry" doesn't take the pain away, doesn't make it better, because nothing will ever make it better except to go back in time and change it.

I cannot begin to express what you mean to me. I only know that you are Home, my Dragon Tear, my lodestar. And I will always be drawn to you, long for you, when we are apart. Do you remember the Dragon Tear? That the last drop of blood from a dragon's heart becomes a shining dark gem, the essence of its spirit.

I feel like the last drop of my heart's blood is about to fall, and that drop is going to hurt so much. I don't know if I'll have a heart left if I make another mistake.

I love you, my precious, Josette

Did I Take Your Life for Granted?

How could I compete given the paltry coffers of my base misgivings, unfounded fears, and self-absorption? After all, you're merely the mirror, not the reflection in it.
NANCY ARNOLD, *Florida*

Dear Mother,
I find myself pondering our relationship daily, usually during the hours between two and three in the morning. I find no answers to the questions I have asked you, myself, or anyone who would listen over the years. In fact, as I grow older, the number of questions multiplies exponentially and their answers avail themselves less and less frequently.

You raised me to be as independent as you, then resented that I never needed you. I cannot say I ever loved you, but I cannot say I did not. Nor can I pinpoint the very act, done or not, the exact word, spoken or not, that made me tend to avoid your touch, dread our telephone conversations, or resent our visits.

It is my own weaknesses at the root of the problem, I fear.

During my early-morning ruminations, I conclude it might be envy. I covet your greater courage, stouter heart, and more generous nature. How could I compete, given the paltry coffers of my base misgivings, unfounded fears, and self-absorption? After all, you're merely the mirror, not the reflection in it.

The competition continues, does it not? Those days I rush and skip breakfast, that little voice says, "How can you function properly without something to stick to your ribs?" As I sit down to lunch, another admonition: "Sweet pickles? I preferred green apples in my tuna salad." As I put dinner on the table, my husband says, "This is great, but you know, no one could make spaghetti and meatballs like your mother." No, nobody.

There were a hundred times in my fifty-plus years when I would have gladly forfeited your life. Ironically, now that I have done so, I am tormented. I didn't murder you, for I know what was in my heart when I signed my name to the termination papers, and the physicians and nurses concurred with my decision. Now I'm a victim of that virulent microbe called mourning that ravishes one minute, then relinquishes my heart the next—one step forward, two steps back. I'm locked in a morbid multistep program: grief, anger, remorse, guilt, and more anger.

My husband snores beside me and the cat purrs at my

feet, but a feeble murmur builds to a deafening scream some-where inside me: "MOMMMMMMEEEEEEE!" Then, in the hush of the early morning, a sensory memory comes to the rescue, that hint of Giorgio perfume, and your final blessing of declared love and forgiveness—given as the morphine drip carried you into oblivion and then beyond. The feeling comes back and wraps around me like an old chenille robe, worn at the elbows and ragged at the hem but warm and comforting. It cradles me until peace takes hold and I sleep again.

It is said one never misses the water until the well runs dry. And our well has run dry, indeed. Yet your example is set before me to amplify your attributes, good and bad, es-pecially the good.

One day, the best in you might prove to exist somewhere in me.

Your loving daughter, Nancy

A Daughter Far from Home

On the one hand, longing for home, you, and being next to you—it's the most difficult part. On the other hand, guilt takes over my thoughts from time to time—a weird feeling that prevents me from enjoying life to its fullest.

DANIELLE NEWMAN, *New York*

Dear Mom,

I'm sorry that I had to grow up and leave you. Our lives have taken different paths. It must have been hard for you when I left, as it was hard for me too. But I never thought that one day you and I would be physically and emotionally apart the way we are today. Everyone used to ask if we were sisters when I was thirteen and you were thirty-two, and we were really good friends. I could tell you everything about my life. I know you dedicated your life to me, and you must think that I take all you did for me for granted. I want to let you know that I appreciated each moment you spent helping me with homework, each time you took me to gymnastics, each time you supported all the positive things I wanted to do.

You didn't support me when I wanted to get a scooter when I was only fourteen. Now I understand why. Actually, I don't know how you stood me when I was a teenager. I was such a spoiled brat. After passing that "teenager crisis" phase, we reconnected again and had that special mutual care for each other.

Then I turned twenty-two years old. One day I woke up and felt that I really had grown up. I started making plans, writing them down, and setting goals for my life without really knowing where I was going to land. The more I planned, the more things took a different route in my life. I was certain about one thing: I felt strongly about accomplishing my goals because you have always told me I could be whatever I wanted. You always trusted me. I know you wanted me to succeed.

I didn't mean to hurt you when I made the decision to come to the United States to study. I didn't leave home because I was unhappy. To the contrary, I just wanted to make you proud of my accomplishments. My experience by myself in a strange country made me really mature. More important, it made me find my true self. Do you remember how scared I was about everything? I was already twenty-one and had to sleep with the hall lights on for fear of the dark. This is all gone because, by discovering myself, I was able to get free from many silly fears.

My experience in the United States was supposed to last one

year, I know, but it turned out to be a much longer journey than we all anticipated. I decided to come back to study more after my first year here. I had also met my husband, Bryan.

You had your life with Dad while it lasted. Unfortunately, you have been apart from each other for almost six years. Please don't blame everyone around you for things you think went wrong. You have so many good qualities; you are compassionate, fun, good company. You care about your family and have a deep relationship with God. I admire you for all you are and all you have taught me.

You just need to reach these qualities from within yourself again to have a fresh start. Why can't you forget the past? No sadness—just love and happiness. We all have to deal with difficult situations because life is a constant challenge. You are still young. Don't let life swallow you up. Find a new partner, find new friends, get involved with a volunteer job, or just travel.

— I am twenty-eight years old; six years have gone by since I left home. I still have mixed emotions in my heart. On the one hand, longing for home, you, and being next to you—it's the most difficult part. On the other hand, guilt takes over my thoughts from time to time—a weird feeling that prevents me from enjoying life to its fullest. Sometimes I catch myself thinking that I don't deserve all the good in my life. I feel guilty about my decision to live abroad. My first year of marriage wasn't easy. I was constantly testing myself and wondering, "Do I really want to stay in this foreign country forever? Do I belong in the United States or in Brazil?"

I almost ran away from my marriage commitment. Patrick, Emanuelle, Dad, and Grandma gave me the necessary support to go on with my life. Nowadays, my guilt is diminishing, but it's not totally gone. I've been married for two years today, November 25, 2002. I'm glad that I decided to proceed with my marriage because Bryan is a wonderful man. Please be happy not only for me, but be happy that your children are healthy, successful, and kind. Show us that you are proud of us.

My biggest dream is to see you happy again: happy with the things that you have, but more important, happy with who you are, because you are a special person. You have always been a good mother, caring, lovely, and beautiful.

This letter goes to you with much love.

Your daughter, Danielle

Disobeying the Truth

*He entrusted me with the secret of his infidelity when I
was sixteen. Am I not forgiven of being disloyal to you,
another woman, only because I was hardly sixteen?*

P. ARGO, *India*

Dear Mom,

How was I to know that, at my age of thirty-five, your every
word would return to me and I would weep to turn the clock
back? At the end, we all succumbed in our separate ways to
the shadow's embrace.

I mourn all the years I wasted resenting you, your success, your career, and your money. All the years I wasted
being loyal to a father who was hardly that. How could I
have been that blind? I feel ill that I aligned myself with his
duplicity against your loyalty, his sponging off you against
your sheer slogging, his philandering against your faithful-
ness, and, ultimately, his dishonesty against your truth. I am
sorry. He was the snake you always called him. You probably forgave me, but the law of karma did not.

I have seen such days when I have scrounged for money. The same money you lavishly spent on me. The same money my father stole so nonchalantly. The same money I hated as the reason that made the two of you incompatible with each other. The same money that kept you from being the ideal wife to him.

I have seen such days when I've struggled to give the best education and exposure to my children that your money gave to me. It was the same money he freely gave to another woman and her son when you were struggling to hang on to your house and to your bittersweet dreams of seeing your children settled and prosperous. I have seen such days when my earnings were so meager, they were less than a fraction of the cost of the weekly dinner and movie you once paid for. Such days when, looking at the faces of my children, I felt the pain and the murderous rage you must have felt when my father betrayed us all, depriving us of the very security we expected from the man of the house.

They accused you of attempting just that—murder—but you were innocent when you would have been fully justified.

Where did I go wrong? I was quiet; you were aggressive. I was reticent; you were more expressive. I was slow; you were fast. I was probably more like my father. I know now there was something very small and self-centered about me in the face of your bigheartedness and dynamism. You were always of the world, grasping life with both hands, refusing to be controlled by hesitation and social restraint. An image of you comes to mind—breaking a cob of corn in a vast field and sinking your teeth into its raw kernels, gorging it in minutes. We all watched, wishing we had the guts to do the same but, in our hearts, thinking you a thief for enjoying something that wasn't yours. It was just one corn on the cob, but no one had given us permission to partake of the field.

My father didn't touch a single cob that day, but touched another woman in ways that pulverized our entire family, our faith in ourselves for years to come. For her, he stole from his wife's pension and his children's inheritance.

You were a marvelous concoction of conservative élan. But let's face it, you told little lies while claiming to be the epitome of truth. I felt each of your little exaggerations deeply. Your stretching of the truth twisted my insides in outrage. And when it was all out that I'd been the custodian for close to ten years of the ultimate lie that destroyed our family, I was suddenly the baby snake—the child of the ultimate snake, my father, the child lying for the liar.

He entrusted me with the secret of his infidelity when I was sixteen. Am I not forgiven for the sheer tenderness of my age? Am I not forgiven for being disloyal to you, another woman, only because I was hardly sixteen? You crucified me for being nothing but Daddy's little girl. You said that I had betrayed your marriage, and that if I had revealed his sordid little secret to you, you could have at least saved your millions. Instead, we were left penniless by his thievery.

Life's greatest irony is that I am more in touch with him than you. Over the years, I have uncovered his deceit, been shocked by it, been numbed, been sensitized all over again, and have learned to separate the man from the deed. There wasn't much of him left. Hardly a snake—a worm perhaps—a pathetic little man biding time. A waste of life too tired to even regret what he'd done—a rubble of dreams. To the world, he looks the victim and you the perpetrator, only because you have bounced back. You are strong and magnificent.

I have wept. I have suffered. I have ached with guilt for having been gifted with a loving husband who is all the things you missed in your husband. I have felt I should have been punished with quite the opposite.

Above all, I have missed you. For my rejection of you in my childhood, karma has denied me you in my prime. From mirror images and cycles of time, I learned that what goes around comes around. I learned to forgive myself and realized there was nothing to forgive in you because you are what you always were: my warm, beautiful, intelligent, lovely, dynamic, adorable mother. Nothing more, nothing less. If I have inherited the best of your genes, my children are lucky. Everyone says I look like you more and more as I grow older. Those who don't understand you look at me and worry at the statement that daughters become their mothers. I hope to God that's true!

With lots and lots of love, your daughter

From Abandonment to Wholeness

The experience of writing to my birth mother, whom I have never met, was very challenging. The only mother I have ever known is the mother who adopted me. As I wrote the letter, I was afraid of not being loyal to her, and yet give credit to a woman for her decision to give up her child for another woman to raise. I began to feel qualities that both mothers had and the love they both had for me.

BARBARA KRAFT, *Wisconsin*

After I finished talking to a group of forty women at a Power-Up Breakfast in San Diego about closure in relationships—especially daughter-mother relationships—a strong-willed woman named Tina stepped forward to speak to me about her mother. I could see that, beyond her guarded appearance, her heart was longing for resolution. Her mother had passed away when she was a teenager, she told me. Since then, she was eagerly trying to put pieces together from her distant memories. Tina said her mother was a frilly, feminine woman, while she herself had been tomboyish as a child. Now, because she felt that her mother misunderstood her, she was searching for validation through counseling and letter writing. And although she believed the therapy helped tremendously, she still couldn't find peace.

The following day, a mutual friend, Sheryl, and I met Tina for some fun. Tina seemed much more enthusiastic, openhearted, and peaceful than the day before. After the Power Breakfast, she had taken time to write a letter to her mother. That's when she realized it was more important to understand her mother than to continue her endless pursuit to *be* understood. As Tina was able to accept her mother and her love, her sense of wholeness was restored.

Many of us have felt the rug pulled from under us. Our mothers (or someone else) unexpectedly abandoned us physically or emotionally. Their rapid departures left us with gaping holes of emptiness and mistrust. We automatically began to define ourselves as inadequate. We guarded ourselves from loving too much for fear that old wounds would resurface.

At the same time, we craved nourishment from others to counter our own insecurities. From young women living in teenage shelters, we learn that no matter how badly their mothers treated them, they still yearn for acceptance and love from them.

"When have you abandoned yourself?" asks Kathleen Potter, psychotherapist and coach for the Letters from the Heart Project™. She poses this question instead of asking about the person who did the abandoning. She explains that "As children, we constantly seek approval from our mothers in exchange for love. Ultimately getting that approval becomes more important than caring for ourselves. If we don't get our needs fulfilled by our mothers or fathers, we continually seek acceptance through others. As a result, we cast aside our own power in the process."

Our initial reaction to Kathleen's question, "When have you abandoned yourself?" might be to defend our turf and point fingers at others. "After all," we rationalize, "they did it to us and that's why our lives turned out this way." Granted, we can't disregard that some mothers left us to fend for ourselves or perhaps were abusive. But we can consistently ask ourselves this question and then identify what truly makes us happy without being blocked by conditioning from our past.

The women who wrote the letters in this chapter moved beyond the barriers of abandonment and discovered the most important lesson of all—not to abandon *themselves*. In a reflective note written months after her first letter to her mother, Elizabeth Grimm wrote, "There is no changing the past. And all things happen for a reason. Because I feel my mother is more accepting of me now, I feel less inclined to force my emotions on her. I no longer feel the need to have her apologize for abandoning me so long ago."

As these women guide us through the most difficult circumstances, they remind us that we can redefine our lives on our terms. It is the spirit soaring within all of us that connects us to the divine self and brings us back to wholeness.

You Left Big Shoes to Fill

Well, Mom, I've made a decision today. I am removing your shoes. I am going to begin life again, this time as me.
JACQUELINE MCMAHON, *Canada*

Dear Mom,
What's happened with our family has left me feeling quite empty. Anna and I have grown so far apart that I really didn't think we were ever going to make it as sisters. Even that term, *sisters*, seems foreign to me. Her life is so different from mine and we think in different ways. I'm sure she has issues as I do that have brought her to this place, but I wish things could have been different. I've had to pull back because I can't keep getting hurt.

Dad is a good, kind, generous man, but having to be the only parent has taken its toll on him in many ways. I don't believe he's ever gotten over losing you to such a sudden death from cancer. But you know him—he doesn't talk about anything. I really don't think he can. The box he has built around himself seems to provide the necessary armor for him to continue without you.

So, Mom, I've been thinking about the way life's circumstances can dictate who we are and who we will become. And I don't know that we can have any control over it. I do know that I have allowed the unfortunate circumstances dealt to our family to take hold over my life in a way that hasn't been productive.

But I have decided to do something about it. I have to figure out a way to step into my own shoes and out of yours. By the way, you sure had big shoes to fill.

Sometimes I do blame you for leaving. I feel like I didn't get a fair chance at figuring out who I would be and living life as *me*. But I was the one who used your absence as an excuse for stepping into your shoes and out of my own.

It isn't you who should be blamed. It's me! I blame me for not seeing what was happening until it was too late. You raised me well. I didn't take my responsibilities to my family lightly, but somehow, I lost myself in the process.

I must admit that I do have regrets. I've waited too long for some things to be possible. I know I'll never be able to give birth to a child, and as I get older, this might be difficult to face. I regret that I lost my sister because I became her mother at a time when she needed both of us and I didn't know how to fix that. I also know that I babied Dad because

he seemed so lonely and helpless. I've made him so dependent on me that I couldn't even think of leaving him on his
own now.

Well, Mom, I've made a decision today. I am removing
your shoes. I am going to begin life again, this time as me.
Somehow, I'm going to find a way to be me and still continue
to be a good daughter. You raised a fighter, Mom. Now I am
going to fight for me.

Love, Jacqueline

You Missed My Wedding

Don't tell me you're "too old" to adjust to having a daughter who loves a woman. Terry's ninety-two-year-old grandmother was the one who proudly walked us down the aisle . . . Grandma Neem says she's too old to worry about the choices other people make.

LAURA LOOMIS, *California*

Dear Mom,

My wedding was beautiful. The only thing missing was you.

Imagine for a moment that my brother fell in love with a wonderful woman. Someone warm, funny, romantic, and absolutely deserving of his trust and respect. You'd have been thrilled. You'd have enjoyed getting to know her and embarrassing him with all the stupid little stories of cute things he did when he was four. You'd have remembered her birthday, sent presents for both of them at Christmas. In conversations, you'd slip and say "the kids" when you meant him, me, and her.

Their wedding would be the highlight of your year.

You'd brag about it to your friends and describe it glowingly in your annual Christmas letter. Their wedding picture would sparkle on your mantel in a silver frame. You'd tell her, "Welcome to the family," and mean it.

But I was the one who fell in love with a wonderful woman.

Terry is all the things I described, and more. She's child-like in the best sense of the word, full of optimism and joy. When I start taking life too seriously, she remembers to play. She told me that I could fulfill my dream of writing a book, and then she sat me down at the computer and told me to start writing. Sharing my life with her is the one decision that I've never doubted.

When we're all in the same room, you're polite to her. You try. But when you call and she answers, all you have to say is, "Can I speak to Laura?" Maybe you never noticed that she tried to keep you talking, hoping you'd accept her once you got to know her. Maybe eleven months after we moved in together, you didn't think about how it would feel when you sent a stack of Christmas presents all with *my* name on them. I don't suppose it felt too good at your end when I called and asked you to at least send her a card. You were embarrassed by your own thoughtlessness. Dad was mad at me for making you cry.

If I'd married a man, any man, you'd have dropped

everything to be here. Even if he were an alcoholic, a criminal, or a Republican.

When you said you weren't coming to the ceremony, I tried to understand, saying it was better to stay away than to come with a black cloud over your head. Why should those be my only choices?

We had everything: a rose garden, Andrew Lloyd Webber's "All I Ask of You," a cake with two brides on top, Terry's family, and my brother. But I had hopes for you.

Don't tell me you're "too old" to adjust to having a daughter who loves a woman. Terry's ninety-two-year-old grandmother was the one who proudly walked us down the aisle. I still get tearful when she introduces me as her granddaughter.

Grandma Neem says she's too old to worry about the choices other people make. And I think, at thirty-five, that I'm too old to worry about that, too. You've missed out on important parts of my life. There's still time to come closer, to keep from missing anything else. But I'm finally realizing that it's not up to me. All I can do is love you even when I wish you'd see it my way.

And I realized something else. It's because of you and Dad that my wedding day was possible at all. You raised me to have faith in my decisions and myself. You taught me that prejudice is wrong, and that's why I didn't go through the angst that a lot of gay and lesbian people do. And you taught me to trust in love. You helped make me the person I am, a woman who could reach out and take the hand of another woman for life.

It's not the life you dreamed of for me, but it's the best life you could have given me.

Love, Laura

Setting a New Example

I gave my daughter our last name. I finally want to break the curse that "Florence Mothers" cannot be there and raise their daughters in loving homes.

LYNN FLORENCE, *Massachusetts*

Dear Mother,

I need to let you know how I feel about my childhood. I need to write this so that I can move on to adulthood at full speed.

I wonder what your childhood was like, if it was as painful and sad as mine was. I think about the times you hit me for telling you, "I love you." I wonder if you were brought up to believe that emotions are a sign of weakness, because that's what you taught me. I think about the times you tried but failed to kill me because my father denied me. I wonder if this is because you and your firstborn share the same father. I think about the times you made promises to me, but didn't keep one of them.

I'll never forget the one and only time you gave me a

compliment. It was the day after your mother died. You looked at me and said to your boyfriend, "Isn't my daughter getting prettier every day?" I remember the look on your face. Like you wanted to say more. Like you wanted to tell me it would be okay. That you were sorry for being an unwilling mother to me. That you should have been the one raising me, not your mother. That you were going to change. That from that point on, you were going to make up for the messed-up first ten years of my life.

Now at age eighteen, I wonder if that was just *me* wishing and hoping for the mother I never had. It's never too late to change.

When I think about you, I feel like that ten-year-old child, wishing and hoping. While I am writing this letter, I believe that it's my last chance to have you as a mother. All I can do is hope that I will be the mother I always wanted you to be. That I show my daughter how to be a good, strong woman. That I show her that no matter what, life goes on, even when life gets so tough that you want to curl up in a ball and die.

My greatest challenge is that I will not be able to let her meet her grandmother because you are nowhere to be found. I'd like you to know, anyway, that I gave my daughter our last name. I finally want to break the curse that "Florence Mothers" cannot be there and raise their daughters in loving homes. My daughter and I will be fine as long as we have each other and remain kind, open, trusting, and loving to each other.

If I had grown up with a good mother, then I would not be in Massachusetts in this shelter. I would have had the love I needed to feel confident in myself a long time ago. I would have finished school, had a decent job, a place of my own. I wouldn't have had my daughter, Laria. But I am thankful to you, Mother, because I've had a taste of the real world, and I have my daughter.

Even though it's a hard path, I've become a very strong person.

Yours truly, Lynn Florence

I Waited Every Day

I figured that you were the only one who could mend my broken heart because you were the one who broke it.
KATELYN WALES, *Texas*

Dear Mom,

Imagine a small, fragile child slumping on the wooden steps of her grandmother's front porch with her arms wrapped tightly around her knees, hoping that *today* her mother is going to return for her. Refusing to play with her dolls, neighbors, or friends, day in and day out, she waits, prays, and hopes. Her ray of optimism quickly fades when cars zoom by without halting. On misty days, she dawdles in her bedroom, staring aimlessly out her dusty bedroom window. And her heart lights up with excitement each time the telephone rings.

Then, one day, tearfully, she realizes that her mother is not coming back for her after all, and all hope turns into anger. She blossoms into a young woman, but there's no mom around to guide her confidently into womanhood. Although she goes on to succeed in life, she feels incomplete because of a grave emptiness inside her and a constant longing for the warmth of her mother.

Mom, although I did not sit on any wooden steps, in my heart, silently, I waited for over twenty years for you to come back and get me. But you never came back. And one day, I realized you were not coming back to make right what was wrong between us.

When I turned eighteen and left home, I thought I could choose my own path, including religion. But the religious path that I chose you could not accept. For reasons that I never understood, you turned on me. Mom, I spent twenty years running from you, even when you were not chasing me. But when I was around you, I did not feel safe. I never wanted or asked you for an explanation. I just wanted to hear you say, "I'm sorry." That's all! And those two small, priceless, and hard-to-say words would have swept away twenty years of high, rough tides of anger, isolation, regret, bitter tears, and hurt.

Your actions completely stunned me because I was very close to you as a child. I was your constant shadow. You were my protector. When you turned on me, it was as though you ripped my fragile heart out with your bare hands and shredded it into a thousand irreparable pieces. One thing that scarred me for an eternity was forbidding me to come home for Christmas the year I was eighteen. At such a tender age, I had to make provisions and take care of myself the best way I could.

Mom, I blamed you for everything that was wrong in my life. For every bad relationship because I didn't have an example to follow. For everything that deals with the feminine issues in my life. For the things I should know about life in general. For the twenty-year void in my heart that I thought only you could fill. For not preparing me for my future when I was a child. For my social anxieties. For the dreadful way my life turned out.

I waited for a letter, a phone call, or even a visit from you. I figured that you were the only one who could mend my broken heart because you were the one who broke it. So I waited, and I waited, and I waited. And you know what? Like the drifting clouds in the sky, life just passed me by. On occasion, I bought you expensive gifts, hoping to renew your love for me. But now I know that true love can never be bought. And although time did heal my wounds, I'm not sure that the bad memories can ever go away. I clearly remember the last time we talked; I had to search for words to say because you have become a complete stranger to me.

You are not responsible for my happiness. I am! It is up to me to either stay bitter or make my life better. And I choose to make my life better. I have the power to choose my thoughts and actions, so I choose to remember the good between us. The best thing you could have done for me was to love me, take care of me, and live your best before me. At some point, you had to let me fly and find my own way. You can only hold my hands for a little while. But if you had been wise, you could have held my heart forever.

Mom, God cares not for our religions, various denominations, strict rules, and rituals. He simply cares that we love Him and one another. I am a grown woman now, and if you never come back for me, just know that I will always love you and that I am okay.

From my fragile heart to yours, Katelyn

You're No Longer My Drug of Choice

Lisa's note: Krina Ulmer and Cheryl Forbes are sisters who independently wrote the following letters to their mom without each other's knowledge.

You are a flame to which I am undeniably drawn. But fire burns and I remember that, too.

KRINA ULMER, *Canada*

Dearest Mum,

The skin is thinning on the back of my hands. It's losing its elasticity and becoming more like the papery covering I know so well on your hands. I see it on my face, too—your skin, your pores, your textures. And the state of my post-pregnancy belly, every stretch mark is like a road map back to you.

I have always carried your resemblance on my skin, but it is now as I enter my thirties that I finally see you. I see the skin of my mother, the mother of my memories rather than the mother I saw in photographs. This is how my daughters will see my skin, will remember the mother of their childhood.

I have missed you. But I have trouble putting my finger on what it is that I have missed until the moment I hear your voice, the moment we lock eyes. Then I remember. I miss your energy, the giddy buzz that flows from your fingers down to your toes. Its hum strikes a chord that resonates inside, and like a drug, it seizes control of my senses, flushes through me, enraptures and terrifies me.

You are a flame to which I am undeniably drawn. But fire burns and I remember that, too.

In the new light of time, I see myself the puppy running amuck looking for choice scraps among your offerings, joyous over any tidbit I was lucky enough to gather. In the mornings when you and Fred were unexpectedly missing, I just carried on as if all were normal. Didn't everyone's parents go away for a "trip" once in a while? Didn't everyone have a twelve-year-old sister and a ten-year-old brother to care for them? I just looked forward to coming home and finding you there. If I was really lucky, you would still be in bed and I could crawl up under the covers and put my cold feet on your back. I was a child who loved her mother completely and unconditionally, and you instinctively cultivated my need for you. I was blissfully unaware of your fallibility.

Then Dad came for us. And like an addict, I knew only the

withdrawal, the emptiness that invaded my life. Those middle years, I lived for the times I got to spend with you. I felt alive when I was with you. I was free to be me, to laugh and talk and be heard. I craved the attention I got from you. Addicted and ignorant, I ran after you. Vulnerable, you filled me with confusion; you spoke hateful things into my life about Dad and I believed you. I never heard the opposing side and so I carried those things around with me. And I hurled them silently at a man who did nothing but try his best to provide me with a stable home, who never spoke ill of you, who only ever wanted me safe and happy. So when the opportunity arose, armed and ready, I chose you over Dad. I stood in the kitchen and watched him cry, lost and helpless, fearful and hurt. He let me go. This vision burns in me.

At twelve, I returned to you. I was happy. But after twelve came puberty and an ugly awareness of truth. I was no longer the young and impressionable child you had so easily entranced. I became a hitch in your plans, a competing force in your world of need. I grew painfully aware that your "needs" were the driving force in our lives, that Fred and I were the tail to your kite—up and down and tossed around trying to stabilize, trying to overcome the bitter winds that seemed to haunt you.

We worked in darkness as you held your demons close, buried, or unacknowledged. But it became harder to pretend

away your behavior, harder to erase the images of your trying to blow hashish smoke up my nose, cleaning up your
vomit Christmas morning, your face missing among the
crowds at award assemblies.

But I filed it all away. I put on a sunny face and moved
forward. Every time Fred touched me, I only thought of you
and how much this would hurt you. So I clung to my own
demons, pushing away truths, building card castles, and
stunning the world with resilience. No one had cause to ask
questions; if they suspected anything, I never revealed
enough to incite them to action. I had perfected my mother's
art for concealing reality with a smoke screen of congenial-
ity. I willingly followed along broken paths, fighting to live
up to my own imaginings.

But as a young adult, you broke me. Your years of acting,
of weaving truth out of fantasy finally overwhelmed me. I
could not withstand the casualness of your acceptance of
what he had done. When you were finally told, when all was
revealed, you took me to a party where you could get high
and forget. You left me alone in the car. No "misplaced" trust
could have hurt me worse than sitting in that car, vulnerable
and abandoned. The potency of your allure caught in my
throat and I walked away. I felt exposed as every lie I had
built up for myself crumbled into dust, leaving only truth
and pain.

Perhaps here is where we part. I broke early. I had only twenty-three years of interwoven lies and hurts and repressed angers to weed through, as opposed to your fifty-plus years. I had the resources to rebuild, to redesign my life according to fresh truths and perspectives. I cried, cursed, and yelled at you in the mirror. I pushed you to the brink of extinction. I wanted you out. But despite it all, I missed you. I mourned for you. I could not move forward without resolving you.

In the end, I have gained new perspectives. As I have become the mother of daughters, I have slowly given you up, given you away as "mother," and assumed the role for myself, revised and renewed. I am no longer a child-daughter and you are no longer my drug of choice. I see that you were a child-mother fighting to free the woman hidden deep within her, buried under layers of hurt, confusion, and fear. You were a woman-child bearing children. You were married, a mother, and divorced before I was the age I met my husband.

Thank you for my skin. I wear it proudly. I could have done without the stretch marks, but at least my girls will always remember they left an indelible mark on me forever.

Love always, Krina

A New Circle

I would dance to your volatile and unpredictable rhythms, waiting for those rare and precious measures when we fell into synch.

CHERYL FORBES, *Canada*

Mom,

Although I was born the daughter, I have been the mother for as long as I can remember. You needed to be cared for, entertained, taught, corrected, and unconditionally loved. I bought your clothes. I helped dress you. I drove you to where you needed to go, made your appointments, and told you I believed in you. Like a child, you simply just stood there when I hugged you. You never knew to wrap your arms around me.

Cleaning up your vomit after days of partying is particularly memorable. You hadn't come home for days and you even missed showing up for Christmas. We were left waiting to participate in our seasonal traditions, and I was left to worry like a mother does about her teenager.

Life went on. I continued to drive you to appointments, sat with you as you recovered from day surgery, and prayed for you to be healed. I gave you your pocket money. I called the ambulance when you needed it, and I forced food into you when you had not eaten in days. I did your hair and makeup for special events. I always tried to show you how pretty you were, and I spoke encouragement into your life. I told you that you were smart when you felt too dumb to speak. I told you that you were lovable when you felt unloved. I told you that you could do anything when you felt stuck. I was there when you felt abandoned. I gave you every emotional, mental, and financial resource I had.

For years and years, I would dance to your volatile and unpredictable rhythms, waiting for those rare and precious measures when we fell into synch. There were a few moments I can remember when you surprisingly did the exact right thing for me, even when I did not know what I needed. I was addicted like a drug addict; the first few hits were free, but then all my days were consumed by trying to get another hit. I wanted more moments, I wanted more understanding, I wanted more mothering.

Coincidently, every time I decided that I would not be a part of your personal chaos, you ended up in the psych ward. Knowing that I could not leave you there alone, I visited. You told me it was because of something to do with me that you did not die or completely follow through. I got so angry with you, disappointed, and hurt, but of course I could not leave you. I ended up telling you I loved you and promising to always be there for you.

Completely consumed by your own tornado of whirling, twirling, manic-depressive drama, I sought shelter. I was the daughter. I wanted a mother. And I could not count on you. Finally, I stopped dancing. I even stopped speaking to you. I walked away and told you never to come after me. I was better off without you than living the idea that you would one day grow into my mother. I was able to understand that much of your craziness was due to your mental illness. Like most bipolar patients, you refused medication. However, without medication, I could not trust you. The more I understood about your illness, the more I understood that much of my childhood and early adult hurts were due to illness, not unwillingness, on your part.

The silent years brought me to a place where I could love you from a safe distance. When I thought of you, I thought of the beauty that always seemed to shine through from the inside, out into the world around you. I realized I believed the things I told you so long ago. You are charming, pretty, caring, smart, and loveable. In these years, I was content to be your secret admirer. I remained steadfast and safe.

Today something changed. Completely unexpected and

without any effort, my paradigm shifted. This very morning, I have stopped wanting you to be more than you are capable of. I may have stopped asking years ago, but it was today I actually stopped wanting you to be anything else but who you are. I stopped needing you to see and understand me more than you can. I stopped hoping you would be fixed so you could be my mother. I suddenly know how to accept you as a woman, unique and not perfect.

At 10:25 a.m. this Saturday morning, I gave birth to my fourth child but my first daughter. Today, I became the woman who is blessed to mother a daughter; no longer am I the daughter who had to mother a woman. Today we can begin a new circle.

Love, Cheryl

The Choice to Forgive

It doesn't matter if she ever acknowledges her responsibility or not. I have accepted the job of creating our future. One day at a time, month after month, year after year, I change how I look at her. She's losing her frightful power and becoming someone I love.

SAVANNAH LATAMY, *Florida*

Several years ago, I gave my first public Heartshop™ seminar at the Wise Women's Weekend for both mothers and daughters. The room was filled with blooming flowers, radiant candles, and soothing smells of lavender. I guided the participants to close their eyes, take deep cleansing breaths, and envision their mothers.

During this visualization, each woman experienced her mother's fragrance, her clothing, details of the environment, and more. They took this opportunity to express feelings silently to their mothers. When they opened their eyes, they captured their individual experiences on paper, leaving their mothers with some final, heartfelt words.

During the discussion that followed this exercise, a beautiful teary-eyed woman eagerly wanted to share her visualization experience but felt stuck in her emotions. All the participants turned compassionately toward her, resonating with the trepidation she felt. Cynthia slowly gathered the courage to share her realization with the group. She said that for years she'd been holding tremendous anger toward her mother for being stoic, unaffectionate, and unloving. She said that her lack of forgiveness toward her created so much pain that she tried to overcome it by showering her own children with love. Yet it was apparent that Cynthia's hurt still hindered her from enjoying the full beauty of life.

After the visualization, Cynthia realized that her mother was a product of her environment, and that she'd done the best she could with what she had. She grasped her newfound insight deeply within. For the first time in her life, Cynthia felt loved by her mother. Her divine transformation from anger and blame to forgiveness uplifted her and everyone in the room.

On that exceptional day, we observed and experienced the miraculous process of forgiveness. Cynthia appeared so much lighter and younger after releasing her pent-up emotions. It was apparent that, as she willingly let go of her grip on resentment, she felt a renewed sense of peace.

We often hear of extraordinary stories like Cynthia's—of dramatic examples of people forgiving their transgressors of horrendous crimes of sexual, physical, and emotional abuse. Yet it can be challenging to even fathom the act of exceptional generosity when our scars go deep. We might continue to blame our mothers, thinking they deserve punishment for their actions. Or we might condemn ourselves for our actions and feelings toward them.

Initially, we want to protect ourselves by keeping our displeasures fresh in our memories. After all, we believe we've been wronged (or have wronged) and are justified in feeling the way we do. But if we probe further into our hearts, we will see that along with our desire to be right, we also hold tight to our judgment, resentment, blame, or feelings of revenge. Beneath our righteousness, we might be eager to let go of our need to punish or be punished, but we keep the anger fresh so we won't forget. And that painful anger eats away at the core of our beings.

The truth is that we can choose to hold on to what chains us—or choose to release it through the process of forgiveness.

Anne Copeland, who wrote a letter to her mother

through the Letters from the Heart Project™, expressed her experience of forgiveness in this profound way: "I feel suddenly as though angels lifted rocks from my soul. What has weighted me down for all the years of my life is suddenly gone as though it never even happened. It is very strange, but I am not kidding. I suddenly cannot remember anything more that is bad at all."

Significant studies and books about the benefits and "how to's" of forgiveness are available, but within them, there's no certain order or method for absolving our mothers. Through the Letters of the Heart Project™, I've learned that, by examining others' processes, their stories of liberation through forgiveness can provide the impetus to start walking on our own paths toward forgiveness.

These writers show us that forgiveness is about letting go of unhealthy attachments and beginning anew. They demonstrate that unconditional forgiveness and love does not necessarily mean unconditional acceptance of others, but the release of the burden from ourselves. Their words encourage us to make viable, positive choices in the moment. Beyond liberation, the blessings of forgiveness lie in our very souls. Letting go ignites the compassion within us and helps us see the humanity in others.

A Child with Two Mothers

You gave me life and a chance for that life to be filled with wonderful opportunities and love. I'm a part of you that was given away, but can always be found.

BARBARA KRAFT, *Wisconsin*

To My Birth Mother,

My life has been one with two lives: one that I have always known and one that I may never know anything about. I have always been a child with two mothers. A mother I always knew and love dearly, and another that I may never know, yet I love as well.

Relatives and friends around me have wondered how I have gone this long without ever trying to find you. The answer is that I have been very much loved and cared for by parents who have only wanted the best for me, and I never felt anything was missing in my life that I needed to find.

I have known other people who were adopted as children, and they harbored a lot of bad feelings toward their mothers. They felt that their mothers didn't love them and certainly didn't want them, or they never would have given them away. My feelings could never have been more opposite.

For never having known you or anything about you, I always had a picture in my head of what you were like. Although I could never see your face, I could envision your heart. It was huge, filled with so much love for a baby girl. Knowing that your heart was so big made me feel that it could only have broken into more pieces than an average-size heart could. I pictured your mind as one filled with thoughts of a little blonde girl filled with love and laughter as she grew older. I hoped that every March 15 you would imagine me as one year older, always being happy and loved just as I was.

A couple had their prayers answered when you entrusted your own child to their care. I often thought how much alike you and Mom must have been. Mom was a woman who always made sure her family's needs were met before her own. She gave unconditionally to family and friends, as well as to strangers in need. She never complained and had an incredible strength for getting through life's toughest challenges. She taught us that we may never be able to change some things in life, but we need to make the best of them.

You taught me the same thing when you made your decision to give me up for adoption. That decision was the hardest one I ever had to face myself. I experienced what you had gone through eighteen years before—what to do with a child that I had become pregnant with. I was not married and had to make a decision of what to do with the child I was carrying. Being raised by a couple who felt blessed by adopting a child of their own, I felt pressured to place my baby up for adoption. I wanted to keep my baby myself. I didn't want either of us growing up to wonder about each other or maybe even forget each other. You possessed strength for making that decision that I never had. I was torn between two mothers on what to do. I didn't want to disappoint either of you by not showing strength to give up a child to another couple praying for one.

My daughter now carries those same genes, and has learned through the love of my mom, how much those traits are a part of who we all are. It is a beautiful thought knowing another good woman will carry on such wonderful traits for another generation.

Our paths in life have never crossed, and although they may never do so, I have felt you in my life many times. Not a birthday goes by that I don't hope that you will remember me, nor a Mother's Day that I don't think of you. I have wondered about you, and who you are, but have never felt it my place to search for you. You have a life separate from mine, and because of your decision, it would be up to you if you'd ever choose to find me. Yes, there will always be a curiosity as to who you are, but I would never want to come in to a family that may not know anything about me. That is your life. You gave me life, and a chance for that life to be filled with wonderful opportunities and love, and it was. I'm a part of you that was given away, but can always be found.

I have come to know the same love and respect that my mom always had for you, by giving us the opportunity to be a family. Just as she taught me, and did herself, I will continue to pray for your peace of mind and heart to know that your unselfish decision to give me up for adoption truly was the best.

Your daughter,

Patricia (I was renamed Barbara when I was adopted)

Holding Your Withered Hands

I can stand tall, knowing that the mirror of life casts a very different picture. I am tender and loving.

SAVANNAH LATAMY, *Florida*

Dear Mom,

Your hands were objects of my fear. Large hands. Strong hands. They could grasp my arm in pain or twist my hair from its roots. They burned as they struck my skin, leaving marks for me to remember you by. Once they swung a hairbrush and broke my front tooth.

"Take my hand, Savannah," you would say to me. Obediently, I would place my hand in yours, not sure if I would be guided through the store as your daughter or your prisoner. When you were displeased, my hand was crushed. Not just my hand, Mom, but my spirit, too.

As I looked into your face, I could see reflections of your heart. It was often an angry and bitter image, and I learned hate by example. I hated you because I thought you hated me. You spoke of your sister with disgust, and there was no love between you. I heard that same tone when you spoke to me.

"Savannah! Why can't you keep your room clean? You're just like your aunt Alice! You're going to grow up to be just like her. You'll never amount to anything. You can't even keep yourself clean! I've never seen her be clean. Look at you. When was the last time you washed your hair? Get into the bathroom now and let me scrub your neck."

Your hands grabbed me harshly, bringing tears to my eyes. I tried to be brave as the washcloth rubbed the top layer of skin away. I was just a little girl, barely even reaching the sink while standing on the footstool. Why did you have to be so rough with me? Were you trying to erase images of your sister? I wasn't Alice; I would never be Alice. Why couldn't you see the little girl that was *me*?

Thank you, Mom, for the things that you taught me. I learned not to hit and cause pain with my hands. I learned not to be devious in a silent infliction of pain. I have been careful not to repeat the exercises that hurt me so much. I learned not to repeat your mistakes.

In the process of evaluating your false impression of me, in the rebellion against that image, I learned who I truly was. I can stand tall, knowing that the mirror of life casts a very different picture. I am tender and loving.

Your hands are old and crooked now. They can't grasp

the jar and remove the lid. They can't hurt me anymore. I have grown and now stand strong. My hands reach out and take the jar from you.

"Let me do that for you, Mom."

I repair broken things around your trailer and we talk about your memories of when I was young. Your memories don't match my memories, but I throw no darts. My life isn't about returning hurts. It is about learning who *you* are today and who *I* am.

Your eyes are clouding, but your heart seems to see more clearly. You still speak Alice's name with a growl, but I no longer hear you call me Alice. Do you know who I am? Have you seen the little girl that remains inside of me yet?

Mom, when you need me, I'll be there. I'll feed you, diaper you, change your smelly linens. I'll look past your inabilities, criticisms, and abusive words. Most of all, I will hold your hands. The hands that frightened and hurt me no longer hold the power over how I see myself. Just like your hands, those old images have withered.

Maybe, just maybe, before you die, you'll see the woman I have become. I hope so. We've already missed so much. Time is passing. I love you, Mom.

Your daughter, Savannah

forgiving Myself for a Broken Promise

*I had to place you in a nursing home when your condition
finally defeated my ability to care for you and keep you
with me. I try to tell myself I have nothing to apologize for.*

LOIS SORKIN, *Illinois*

Dear Mom,
How could I have done this to you? Over all the years of
my life, you have been an unbelievable source of light and
inspiration. You somehow knew how to be the perfect
mother in a generation that was never even taught how to
parent. You absorbed your hurts and cushioned mine. You
were compassionate, funny, and strong. You even supported
me when I slipped into and used against you the generation
gap. And in later years, when we closed it—when we
learned to treat each other as contemporaries—we had an
enriching and always positive relationship. We attended social and cultural events together. We were able to have fun in
places where everyone else seemed bored. And like college
kids just discovering their own ability to concretize unfath-

omable abstractions, we even toyed with uncovering the meaning of life.

You were right. This life is not what it first seems to be; it is not what we thought it would become; it does not progress as we assumed it would. It is a perpetually changing screen, and we have no pause control. Just when we think we can dictate which of its countless elements will remain in the background and which will rise to the fore, the scene shakes itself up and our world changes beyond recognition.

Once during those discussions, I compared life to a perpetual party in which the guests—for reasons beyond their control and often in circumstances beyond their comprehension—are taken away, one by one, while the festivities are still in full swing. They are given no choice; their ride has come for them.

You liked my analogy, but you pointed out that the party changes over the years. The menu changes. The music changes. The participants change. The words change. The rules change. The games change. And you suggested that some people may even want to leave the party before their ride comes. For them, the old games have lost their appeal, and they're unable to play the new ones.

It seemed to me for years that you could never be touched by the phasing-out process. You never struggled with health or memory, and you were never confounded by your evolving circumstances. You were the digression in your own pattern. You spoke the new language, played the new games. And you had always kept pace with the changes, both internal and external, that caused other families to disconnect. You maintained a discreet distance when distance was appropriate, and you were always there when closeness was needed. When I married and moved away from home, you graciously stepped aside and took a different place in my new life; you had a flawless instinct for your changing maternal role. And you stepped back in as my best friend at just the right times.

But, Mom, there was just one incongruity in this perfect picture. You always told me—all my life—and I never knew why you even brought it up, "Don't ever put me in a nursing home." I never understood why you would think of saying such a thing. Why would I? How could I? It was out of the question. I never even gave it any serious thought.

Now I am forced to revisit my own analogy and take a closer look at the people who are ready but still waiting—often in silent desperation—for their rides to come. When we concocted that image, it was nothing more to me than an intellectual exercise.

But you can no longer play any of the games, neither the new ones nor the old. Your powers of expression—once so ready, so sharp—have all but left you, and you struggle to find words that are no longer there. For you, that flippant metaphor has become reality.

"Don't ever put me in a nursing home."

During all those years, you must have sensed something you never shared. Some private instinct, some fear of the future that you kept to yourself.

Now I sit with you in the forbidden place and wait for your final ride. It's a grim way station. It's not a place that restores or supports life; the caregivers do not perform magic. When you call out in pain, they snap back, "Don't make so much noise. You're disturbing the others." What else can they do? You can no longer tell them or even show them where it hurts, and the truth is, they don't much care. They can never experience or imagine the person you were. At any rate, to them it is irrelevant.

"Don't ever put me in a nursing home." I tried in every way possible to give you a life in my home with my family. Your mother died in her own home, and your father, in yours. I never wanted you to be so utterly alone. But I had to place you in a nursing home when your condition finally defeated my ability to care for you and keep you with me. I try to tell myself I have nothing to apologize for. The nursing-home issue emerges simply as one of those shifting background elements that have caught us unaware.

"Don't ever put me in a nursing home." I always thought

you were talking about abandonment, and of course I would never abandon you. Now I understand you were pleading, "Never let me descend to that level of degradation." And I'm counting on you to understand that Alzheimer's is life's most dastardly prank. I was helpless to prevent it.

I will never even jokingly direct my children never to put me into a nursing home. This was perhaps your only noticeable mistake. But, Mom, it's okay; you have taught me to cope with impossible situations. And I know your judgment was always governed by understanding and tempered by forgiveness.

In spite of everything, your eyes still light up when I come to visit you, and I believe that even though you can no longer say so, you have forgiven me. *My job now is to forgive myself.*

It was easier to live with the facile metaphor of a perpetual party when it was nothing but a junk pile of intellectual catchwords—and before I was forced to understand what it all really meant.

I will always love you, Lois

No Longer the Cause of All That's Wrong

*I can forgive the errors made in the past, but I can't write
a blank check. Wouldn't that be giving you permission to
hurt me over and over again?*

VICTORIA STREIB SMITH, *Georgia*

Dear Mom,

It hasn't been easy being your daughter. For many years, I
shared our stories with others in order to make sense of my
life and to learn to trust my own perceptions. During that
time, I cherished a righteous anger and saw you as the cause
of all that was wrong in my life. If only you would admit to
your errors, I would consider forgiving you. Odd, that the
harder I pressed you to "fess up," the harder you resisted.
Over the years, I came to realize that despite all you had
done wrong, I would need to forgive you unconditionally or
forever live in the thrall of those stories.

When I first tried on this concept, I was stymied. I remember thinking, "I can forgive the errors made in the past,
but I can't write a blank check. Wouldn't that be giving you

permission to hurt me over and over again?" But then I looked at how frequently I resolved to change my own patterns and still would see myself repeat them. I too need the compassion of forgiveness in order to change. Perhaps it was the same for you.

The need to cultivate forgiveness for myself became clearer when I had my own private war, after landing in the maze of mental illness. Throughout my young adulthood, I had prided myself on my own sanity, thinking that I had built it by prevailing against you, through a good strong will and self-honesty. My recovery made me realize that my sanity was a God-given gift, not my ego's creation. It was then when I was on my knees, unsure if I would ever find a path back to my self, that I realized I could not afford to fight you any longer. I had no energy to coerce you into giving what you could not give.

It didn't matter what you had done in the past to hurt me. So you had taken out your frustrations on me. So you had not given me a key to the home I grew up in. So you had taken credit for my accomplishments and told me that I would never amount to anything without you. I had to let go of each of my angry stories in order to live in the present. In the end, it was me I had to forgive—for thinking I could make you love me in the way I needed.

Once I was forced to put my own healing above any arguments, I came face-to-face with the big knot in my own

heart. The very joy and flavor of my life depended on my unraveling that knot, to create room for forgiveness. I needed
to witness and honor my own pain, but not fan the flames of
resentment in the process.

Maybe you knew that you couldn't help. You called me
only once during that long year of rebirth. It was when I finally came off all the medications that you called me again.
"I have been praying for you," you said with some sense of
accomplishment. Once I might have reacted with, "How
dare you take credit for my recovery?" But how could I
know that your prayer had not helped? Perhaps you had had
your own liberation—and you were admitting to me that
prayer was all you really had been able to do for me. Why
could I not just share your happiness?

For I had said my own prayers during those many
months. When my anger and fear would arise and you would
not call, I was advised to pray for you. I had resisted and initially could only pray for you to change into what I needed.
Gradually, it felt more peaceful to pray for you with no
strings attached. "Dear God, help her find a path that suits
her need even if I do not recognize it." And finally, "God, I
ask you to forgive my mother; allow me to see her humanity
and not expect more of her than she has already given."

The first seeds of forgiveness sprouted when I was not
looking. When I discovered my first peace with you, I

thought, "Forgiveness at last!" I wanted to share the nourishment, not realizing it was only the immature fruit of the first season. I told you that "I had forgiven you." You rebuked me, saying, "How dare you throw those words in my face?" I had been arrogant enough to say I had forgiven you, as if it were a process that I had completed. Now I know it continues as long as I live.

I thought I was only allowed to love myself when you had given me permission. And so, I would fix each phone misunderstanding with a carefully written letter, in which I was a good and honest daughter. You never believed a word. When I saw how much I rejected myself without your help, I knew that trying to get you to love me was a misplaced use of energy. I had yet to learn to love myself despite your criticisms and rejection. As I started claiming myself as a writer, I learned to stop blaming you for my own insecurities. Even your snide remarks need not affect me. I learned that many of your attacks were not even real if I took care of myself and my beliefs about myself. When an unresolved button got pushed, I got myself off the phone so I could reflect on my new homework assignment.

There are so many threads I have pulled through this quilt that I can no longer see where it all began. I have come to enjoy stitching—sometimes it's embroidering, sometimes repairing. What is important is that the quilt has become a thing of beauty because of the very tears and rends we have both mended. So you see, I cannot point to a set of steps I've taken that led to this peace between us. I only know that the old places in my heart that used to hurt are no longer raw.

Forgiveness works its magic without my ever having to say a word to you about my own small role in it.

Love, Victoria

Packing Your Bags for Your Trip to Hospice

Although I haven't forgotten all the unpleasant memories, they have faded like a baseball cap left in the back window of the car for the summer. I have forgiven you.
HEATHER LARSON, *Washington*

Dear Mom,

I watched as you packed for what turned out to be your last adventure. You chose the ugly, faded brown suitcase with tan stripes, the one with sturdy, rigid sides and a chipped handle. When you first opened it, memories of your travels to Australia, Russia, and Belize came wafting out on the scent of mothballs.

You placed two neatly folded nightgowns next to your nylon underwear, then added a few toiletries, as if you were packing for a vacation. You gently slipped your eyeglasses into the side pocket, although months of chemotherapy had permanently blurred your vision and made those glasses useless. I resisted the urge to tell you not to take them.

Then you collapsed back into your wheelchair and clutched your purse into your lap. You let out a sigh that momentarily drowned out the rattle of the oxygen tank that helped you breathe. *"Ticktock, ticktock,"* roared the clock over the fireplace.

I wanted to ask you the litany of questions running through my mind, but you couldn't have answered me. Pneumonia had paralyzed your vocal cords.

I closed my eyes and wrinkled my forehead to conjure up a vision of you returning home with that same suitcase full of dirty clothes. We needed to talk about so much. But I knew our conversations were over. You must have known, too. Your eyes mirrored a terror I'd never seen there before and you reached out for my hand. Touching others didn't come easy for you. While I was growing up and into my adult years, touching and hugging had always been reserved for very special occasions.

Perspiration plastered wisps of gray hair to your cheek. You fidgeted and twisted in your wheelchair, which made tiny squeaking sounds. Your hand felt warm and moist when it squeezed mine. Finally, a hollow knock on the front door signaled that the ambulance was outside waiting to take you to the hospice center.

You were never the kind of mother I wanted or thought you should be. I don't think you knew how to be a mother because you didn't have your own role model to follow. Your mother spent her life trying to please men instead of nurturing her own children.

I remembered, when I was eleven years old, going into the bathroom and finding blood in my panties. You were in the living room watching television. "My period started," I cried out. I had been waiting for months and months for this long-awaited yet terrifying event. Mothers knew what this meant to a young girl better than anyone. I wanted your comfort and advice. Instead, you handed me a book you had gotten in the mail from the Kotex company and then raced to the bathroom. I heard you retching and vomiting. When you finally returned, you dismissed my news and me by asking Dad to take me out to dinner. Were sexual issues so hard for you to face?

You argued with and yelled at my dad constantly. Did you ever know how to love him? I hated spending my weekends at home when I was a teenager because your threat of committing suicide always hung in the air. I worried constantly while you spent Friday night to Sunday night locked in your bedroom, weeping and whimpering. Sometimes I wondered if you were ever coming out.

Your reaction to my pregnancy during my second year of

college didn't seem motherlike either. You found out about my pregnancy by reading a personal letter hidden in my dresser drawer. Then you threw your good china dishes at me, yelling, "You're a slut! Are you proud of yourself?" Dad moved me into a hotel until I could find a job and rent an apartment. I miscarried that pregnancy and the next one, as well. I punished you by not telling you about my second pregnancy, and in my heart I blamed you for the first.

Years later, when I was properly married and the mother of two, you surprised me by being the perfect grandmother. I felt so lucky that, unlike other mothers I heard about, you didn't give me advice on mothering my children. You loved my kids unconditionally and delighted in every moment of their growth. You begged to see them often and they never seemed to be too much for you. Telling your friends about the cute and clever things your grandchildren did highlighted your days.

I really struggled with what to say while you lay dying in that hospice bed. My "I love you's" came from my heart, but seemed so inadequate. I'm not comfortable with one-sided conversations, so I tried alleviating your fears by reading you portions of my autograph book. We did have some great memories to savor.

Your face brightened when I read you parts of my child-hood diary, especially the parts about boys I liked and the trauma they caused me. But most of the time, I just sat by your bed writing in my journal. I sensed a closeness we never had before, plus you seemed more at peace when you opened your eyes and I was the first one you saw.

Why did you have to be on your deathbed before our relationship could mend?

For the first couple of years after you died, I typed letters to you on my computer so I wouldn't go crazy. Still, sometimes when I find out something I want to share with you, I run to the phone and start dialing your number. Then I remember you have an unlisted one.

I am communicating with you now better than we ever did when you were here because I don't see that judgment in your eyes and your body language. Even though you can't vocalize your thoughts, I feel your presence and imagine what those thoughts are.

Although I haven't forgotten all the unpleasant memories, they have faded like a baseball cap left in the back window of the car for the summer. I have forgiven you. I know now that I wanted what you didn't know how to give me, but easily bestowed on my children.

If I get a chance to pack my suitcase before embarking on my last adventure, I'll bring photos of my grandson, Elias, to show you. You'll find him irresistible.

All my love, Heather

The Courage to Grieve

*When she died, the rabbi gave me permission to enclose
the letter in her casket. I read it to her privately before I
placed it in the casket. I also read it at the funeral service.
It was easily the most difficult thing I've ever had to do,
but when I finished, I was enveloped in an incredible
sense of peace and closure.*

SHERRI GOODALL, *Oklahoma*

When something dreadful happens, you may think, "A moment ago things were not like this; let it be *then*, not now, anything but *now*. And you try and try to remake *then*, but you know you can't. So you try to hold the moment quite still and not let it move on and show itself." These are Mary Stewart's thoughts, expressed in her book *Nine Coaches Waiting*.

I've felt this tug-of-war of emotions many times in my moments of despair when I'd prefer to ignore the obvious lump in my throat rather than deal with the wrenching pain of my tears, especially when conversations around me were about death as we watched my mother, hooked up to life-support machines, not knowing if her brain or heart were intact.

I realized that grief is not wrapped in a neat package waiting to be opened. It comes barreling at us like an earthquake, shaking our very core, leaving us helpless and vulnerable. We don't know what to do with the mosaic of feelings associated with an anguished heart. Our tempestuous relationship with grief has us begging for it to reveal itself while, at the same time, rarely giving us permission to do so.

Frightened and uncomfortable in our darkness, we convince ourselves that it isn't appropriate to let go. We search endlessly for shortcuts to bypass the inevitable. The more we suffocate the fear, the more deadened we feel. Grief forces us to surrender, fall to our knees, listen, and examine every piece of our heart.

At the time, I would have done everything to reverse the agony of almost losing her. When she was recuperating, I panicked every time she stayed home alone or didn't tell me where she was. The ironic part was that I actually thought I could control her fate. But she felt my apprehension and summarized it by saying, "We all must die one day," and "It's between God and me," and "I don't fear *anything* after all I've been through."

It doesn't matter if our relationships are stormy; a mother's death changes the course of our lives forever. In Hope Edelman's survey for her book *Motherless Daughters,* 56 percent of the women stated that losing their mothers was one of the most significant events in their lives. Edelman wrote, "The daughter mourns not only what was lost, but what will never be—and if her mother didn't offer protection and support when alive, the daughter also grieves for what she once needed but never had."

Recently, a father from Mississippi was searching desperately for his daughter to let her know about her mother's passing. He did a search on the Web for her name and the Letters from the Heart Project™ popped up. Before responding to him, I read his daughter's letter again. I quickly discovered that she had expressed her disappointment in her mother for not standing up to her father's physical abuse. She chose to leave home, never to come back.

Knowing that, I never gave the father her contact information, but promised to call and let her know about her mother's passing. When I heard back from her, she said she and her mother had disconnected from one another a while ago, but she did want to know when and how her mom had died. When I found out this information, I was able to give it to her, knowing that she had reconnected with her mother in spirit. She decided to have a memorial ceremony in her mother's honor every year.

Some women whose letters appear in this chapter had tumultuous relationships with their mothers and learned more about their mothers and themselves during the time of their mothers' passing. Others who were young when their mothers passed on only have old photographs with which to piece together their lives. Some miss their mothers terribly; others feel even closer to their mothers after their passing because the nuances of physical life have disappeared.

Most important, each one came to understand the relationship better and could therefore experience peace with the one who gave her life. As Heather Larson noted, "Although I never had a good relationship with my mother when she was alive, I feel that I have a great one with her now that she has passed. I can concentrate on the happy times we had together and not worry about the negative."

We've been told that "time heals all." Yet time doesn't heal unless we *choose* to let it heal us through grieving. If we deny and fight the process, we become stuck in the agony of the past. Beneath the grief are the treasured emotions of the heart; therefore, it's essential that we let each emotion blossom fully. We may think of grieving as the mourning of a physical death, but it accompanies any loss we experience in life: a powerful emotional process designed to wake us up to what is most essential.

The letters from the women featured in this chapter can give us the courage and honesty to become fully aware of the depth of our wounds—and to honor death or any loss in a more graceful way. They remind us that it is possible to discover jewels on the road to the unknown. And in embracing our uncertainty and strife, we can regain our feelings of vitality.

What I know is that we're all profoundly connected to one another and traveling to the same destination. As my mother's near-death experience reminded me, within the flicker of life and death lie our most valuable moments. What we do with these fragile moments of time is pivotal to the direction of our voyages.

As you glimpse into these women's experiences in the following letters, I hope they encourage you to transform your thoughts into what's important *now*. The truth is this: It's never too late to connect with your mother and resolve your differences. Your relationship with her never dies; it lives inside forever.

If Only We Had More Time

If only you could have held on past your death at fifty-six . . . you would have known a granddaughter. We all would have embraced and danced in a circle—over the rooftops, above the clouds of gloom, and into the sun . . .
GLORIA G. MURRAY, *New York*

Dear Mama,

I try to remember you before the gloom came and settled like fallout over the rooftop of our Brooklyn apartment, when you proudly wore the gray Persian lamb [coat] Daddy bought you (the one time he *splurged*), when you took me to the Loew's Pitkin Theatre with your best friend, Eva, the lady with a Hungarian accent and Mr. Potato Head ears, and bubbly Aunt Bea, your sister who lived upstairs. I sat between their padded bosoms in my Buster Brown shoes, hair tied back in frizzy braids, eating Raisinettes and swinging my skinny legs across the seat.

There was a time when you sang in your soprano voice, swooning to Mario Lanza—a time before the gloom came and invaded you like an alien, poked out your eyes, replaced them with dark birds of scattered fear, took your wide scarlet smile, and sewed it into the jagged line of a scarecrow's mouth. The alien lived in your body, dragged your swollen spider-veined legs across the room, and uttered strange sounds from your lips.

Mama, how could I have known, understood the life you hungered for with the musician with the clubbed foot you almost married but didn't because Grandma said you'd "shame" the family, the piano that stood silent without the stroke of your slender fingers?

If only you could have held on past your death at fifty-six when a clot burrowed like a small animal in your brain, you would have known a granddaughter. We all would have embraced and danced in a circle—over the rooftops, above the clouds of gloom, and into the sun.

Your daughter, Gloria

Your Loss Has Become a Gift

We will meet again; this I know. And since we have all of eternity, there is no need to hurry, is there?
ROSE STAUFFER, *Virginia*

Dear Mom,
A mother's love knows no boundaries or dimensions.

We have always loved each other, but our spiritual journeys led us apart in those years before your death. You struggled silently with your pain and losses from cancer; I struggled silently with my fears and emotions about embracing my own spirituality. The example shown was not to expose and reveal all the ugly, angry emotions and thoughts to anyone. Not even to one's family. I kept my inner world completely separate from you, and that exclusion carried me deeper into isolation from myself. Despite your many met and unmet goals, you left this world quietly without protest, unobtrusively, so as not to bother anyone, not even your family. Did you leave that way out of cowardice, passiveness, peace, love? For many years, I couldn't figure that out.

In truth, I wouldn't say I ever felt abandoned, although all the books on psychology and bereavement would say that I did. I do not resent death, and my beliefs about death run very differently from those of the world. You did not abandon me, Mom, and I know that because I have learned to sense and feel your presence in my life in many ways. I miss your physical form, your soft, open arms and penetrating looks, but in reality, your early departure from my life has proven to be an immense gift, in light of all the ways I've grown as a result of that loss.

After your death, your role in my life was transformed. No longer limited to the dogma and paradigms of your religious affinities, I began to experience you as a guiding presence.

Since your passing, my life has truly expanded into all it was meant to be, and I feel so grateful and intrigued by the spiritual growth process. I am utterly vexed and stymied not to share it with *you*, my mother, my heart, my source! Everything I've come to know about being a woman in these forty years traces around to you, dear soul, and you're not here in the flesh to reflect it back! Yet I know you have helped me mother my own daughter, to be a parent, to raise her in unconditional love and freedom.

So this is what I do. I smile and breathe deeply with nature, Mom, because you instilled in me a love of the natural world. As far back as I remember, you noticed sunsets, flowers, scenery, mountains, oceans, the wind in the trees, the moon, the song of the birds. I like to imagine that you would be painting again, like you did when we were young children, watercolor landscapes of the natural world.

I also visit with you, Mom, when I read and write, for these were your treasured pastimes, too, and where you'd go to center yourself. I can see you with devotional books, pen and paper, sitting on the verandah in the cool morning hours, by yourself. When I do these things, too, I feel your breath on my shoulder, your smile in my heart, your warm brown eyes shining with love and pride.

We will meet again; this I know. And since we have all of eternity, there is no need to hurry, is there?

Love, Rose

This Too Shall Pass

Can you hear the quiet tears that fall on my pillow when I have dreams about you that are so real that I yearn not to awake?

AMY CZARNECKI, *Utah*

Dear Mom,

Can you hear me when I tell you that I miss you so much that I ache? I've missed you every day since you have been gone. I miss your smile, especially when I was the one that put it on your face. I miss your laugh and all the times we laughed together. I miss your voice, even when the words were not what I wanted to hear.

Can you hear the quiet tears that fall on my pillow when I have dreams about you that are so real that I yearn not to awake? I dream of the days when I was a child. When I look back now, I finally realize how much you sacrificed for my happiness. I dream that you are still here. Those dreams remind me of how good it was to have you in my life, and how hard it is to let you go.

Can you hear me laugh when I share the stories of our favorite moments together? Countless times I have shared how my mother started mashed-potato fights at the dinner table. Every Christmas, my sister and I reminisce about the many wonderful holidays we spent decorating the tree, our house, and homemade cookies with you.

Can you hear my heavy sigh when I realize there is no more time left for us to create new memories? Although you are in my heart forever, we will never again be able to hug, dance, laugh, or celebrate together like we did when you were here. Never again will I call you in the middle of the night, just so you can tell me that everything that is going badly in my life will sort itself out.

If you can hear me, please tell me once again, "This too shall pass." Tell me that the pain of Christmas without you will pass. Tell me that the pain of knowing you will miss out on being a grandmother to my children will pass. Please, tell me that the pain of losing you will pass.

I miss you, Mom, with all my heart.

Forever your daughter, Amy

God, Why Is She Suffering?

There is a hint of curl in the back [of your hair]. The two of us came up with the nickname Curly-Q for you.
VICKIE ANN JENKINS, *Oklahoma*

To my dear, sweet Mother,
I am writing this letter to you as I sit at your bedside. You fought a battle of cancer for fourteen years, and now you are bedridden. I sit with you often, feeling a real need and want to take care of you. I know that you are aware of my presence, yet your warm body remains motionless.

I reposition the pillows under each arm, straightening the white sheet that covers your legs. The cancer has spread throughout your body and is beginning to spread to your brain and to your liver. Your hands are puffy and swollen. I touch each of your fingers, and your once baby-soft skin is now rough with dryness. The color of your skin appears irregular with redness scattered randomly over your body. Your face seems almost ashen. Your hair, which has finally grown to almost an inch in length, is gray in color. There is a hint of curl in the back. The two of us came up with the nickname Curly-Q for you. "You can just call me Curly-Q now," you told me a few weeks ago. We laughed at that. You are so proud of your hair. After all, this is the fourth time that it has grown back from losing it to the chemotherapy.

I know that you are dying. My heart aches. There are words of encouragement from friends, yet sometimes I find myself questioning God. God, why is my mother so sick? Why did she get cancer? Why is she suffering so much? Why?

Now it seems like this is all a bad dream and I want it to end. "Oh God, let your will be done," I pray. "Don't let my mother suffer anymore. Let your will be done. Amen."

I think it is ironic that you spent the early days of motherhood taking care of me, only to find that the roles are reversed as I take care of you. Once again, I fluff the pillows beneath your head, trying to make you as comfortable as I can. I think I catch sight of a smile as the corners of your mouth turn upward ever so slightly when I spread a special ointment on your lips. Or perhaps that is what I see. I know that the time for you to go away is growing near.

Tonight there is a special feeling in the room. I feel God's presence all around as the angels surround us. I feel myself drawn closer to your side. I look at you, my dear, sweet mother of seventy-four years, and it's as though every moment that we had ever shared dances through my mind. I know that it is time for you to go, to let the angels surround you, and to let you go to be with Him.

Now, I am the one who has to let go. Tears run down my cheeks as I finish writing and reading this letter to you. I know it will be the last time we will feel that special bonding between us. I give you a kiss and hold your hand, tightly clasped within mine. It is the same feeling that I had when I was little, and you held my hand within yours. Do you remember? I will never forget the feeling of being cared for, knowing that everything was all right.

It is time . . . through tear-filled eyes and a trembling voice, I give one last whisper of words, "Mother, I will always possess that special love that only you and I share. I love you, Curly-Q. You need to let go now."

Minutes later, a peaceful look came over your face, a look that told me that you understood the letter that I had just read. With calmness, you took your last breath, and with a sigh of relief, I knew that the angels had taken you. I felt God's presence and knew that you were at peace. Reaching over, I turned off the oxygen machine. The tranquility that came over the room captured my heart.

I will think of you often, Mom. Remember this last letter and be thankful for the years that God allowed us to be together.

Love, Vickie Ann

As Unpredictable in Death As in Life

Yours was a miracle that turned me around. The same cancer that devoured your body and took you away from your husband and sons made me—your only daughter—see you as a woman who lived a life, and not just as the mother who complained about mine.

EVE NICHOLAS, *Texas*

Dear Mom,

I'm having a hard time making sense of this. First, for a period of time that lasted for thirty-one years, you and I couldn't be in the same room together without fighting and rolling our eyes. Then, after your diagnosis, we got along famously, waving to each other through doorways, talking about ice cream and chemotherapy, living-room furniture, and colors to paint your walls. While the change was sudden, it wasn't shocking. You were dying, after all, and rather quickly at that. Something about it made you become incredibly honest and quite pleasant to be around.

But now that it's over and I have some time to think, I'm perplexed. You were as unpredictable in your death as you were in your life. I'm happy about that, for once, because we finally enjoyed each other. But at the same time, it makes me feel like I know even less about who you were and what kind of woman you wanted me to become.

I dream about you almost every night. Sometimes I see your belly tucked into blue jeans; other times I see your hand holding a pen and writing a note. One night I dreamt you were in a swimming pool, holding the side, your shoulders freckled from the sun and your eyes behind glasses so big that your cheeks were hard to find. Last night I dreamt that it was my turn to take care of you, but instead of going right to your house, I stopped somewhere and danced in a room by myself. You rose out of your bed to find me, looking sicker than I've ever seen you. When you found me, you raged violently, your arms flailing, your face red from being breathless.

Here's something that I don't understand. How is it that you found grace on your deathbed, that you didn't rile in terror, praying to God to let you live one more day? This is what I would have expected from you—the volatile, moody mother I knew in my childhood, the one who shouted so loudly that I cowered behind doorways, slinking back to my room.

And here's something else. If I liked you so little, why did it break my heart when you told me what the doctor said? Why did it take my words away, and why did you wait until that conversation to be quiet and listen to the sounds I didn't make? We sat there in silence and waited until we were ready to talk more.

Miracles happen all the time. Big ones, like babies who are born to mothers who didn't think they could pull it off. And little ones, like red wine stains that wash out of table-cloths. Or homemade haircuts when the bangs don't turn out crooked or too short. And then there are the unfortunate miracles, big and small, that bite you on the backside just to make you turn around.

Yours was a miracle that turned me around. The same cancer that devoured your body and took you away from your husband and sons made me—your only daughter—see you as a woman who lived a life, and not just as the mother who complained about mine.

I've heard people talk about "good deaths," the kind when your family is all around you and everyone says what they need to say, when your body isn't reeling in agony and you don't go haywire or slip into a coma for too long. I don't know much about death, but I think yours was a good one, Mom. Your hair looked just right and your lips, when you reached them forward, puckered like a little girl's. It made me search in my purse for a Chapstick, which I smeared immediately across your mouth.

I don't know much about your life and, to be honest, I don't feel like I have a very clear perception of my own. I didn't like you at all really, until just before you died. Even then, it wasn't my doing. You opened the door and welcomed me in.

But one thing I do know is that something extraordinary and triumphant happened before you died. Maybe God did it to you, or the act of dying, or maybe you did it by yourself. But in two short weeks, you transformed my understanding of life and time; you showed me that love thrived in a place that looked and felt barren; and strangely, you gave me an exquisite example of how to die—one that makes me want to follow in your footsteps.

The whole thing from your diagnosis until your death took a total of two weeks and one day. Here's something you taught me: Two weeks and one day is more than enough time to take care of most things. Cemetery plots can be purchased. Funerals can be planned. Estates can be changed, possessions can be given away, and whole relationships can be recreated, no matter how complicated they were up to that time. Which makes me question the thirty-one years of my own life that led me up to this point. *Love* can transform two weeks and one day into the greatest two weeks and one day of an entire life.

From your daughter, Eve

Realizing Love

Love in the beginning and love in the end. Never lose sight of love. Even if you don't feel love in the entire region of the heart, in your entire head, in your entire being—let there be a tiny spot, just one tiny spot in your being that throbs with love. Never let it vanish. Never cover it up or stifle it. Always stay in touch with it. Let it fill your eyes.

SWAMI CHIDVILASANANDA, *My Lord Loves a Pure Heart*

What is it to know and feel love as you have always known it? What is love?

My blank page stared back at me and finally whispered, "It is the eternal, divine space between and within everything—the miracle within all of us. To know it is to feel infinite wholeness. To define it is to limit its essence.

To capture a glimpse of it is to fully breathe in the emotions of life."

Princess Diana delivered this message to millions of people as she fully gave her heart to the world. Her courage and openness to step off her throne and share her suffering liberated others to feel the vulnerability of their own emotions. Her story of a shattered princess broke the false image of the perfect palace. Her need to feel loved echoed our own need to love and feel loved. On the day of her tragic death, she moved the entire world into a deeper state of compassion and intense love. This princess gave us the gift to experience our feelings without reserve.

Our lifelong quest is to find our way back to the eternal light from which we are born. Everything we feel and do comes out of how we experienced this love or how we perceived its absence. We can fear our pain so much that we hopelessly search for love, worshipping everyone and everything except ourselves. Our desire for instant bliss keeps us stuck in an illusion of love that simply doesn't exist.

Tibetan Buddhists believe that all beings were once our kind mothers in other lifetimes, even if they seem to be our adversaries now. Believing that our emotions are our rivals, we tiptoe around them, thinking that's the easiest way to live. We desire acceptance most, yet we keep on rummaging for it in all the wrong places. The only way to discover it again is to experience and trust every moment, to feel *through* our anger, shame, guilt, sorrow, and fear of abandonment.

If we avoid facing our own truth, we continually create our own limitations, our own form of inner chaos. We find ourselves back in the same place over and over again. Yet if we gently acknowledge and trust our feelings in spite of the uneasiness, we can move through our fears more fluidly to greater possibilities.

About her experience of writing to her mother, Courtnea Stark said, "I could finally tell 'my story' as I lived and felt it, rather than having it interpreted by someone else. These were my words and my feelings as only I could have felt them. Now I can easily express other events that have occurred in my life without fear of someone else correcting or chastising me for my telling the truth. I have always been afraid of being punished for telling my story. Somehow, now, I don't have that fear anymore."

All of the women who participated in the Letters from the Heart Project™ had an intense need to express their feelings to their mothers. Some have always had a great mother-daughter relationship and wanted to express their love in words through the process of writing a letter. Others released their negative emotions and found their way back to loving their mothers.

As these heroic women committed themselves to the path

of healing, they cultivated their emotions as springboards to go beyond their suffering. By forging through their conflicts, they encourage us to forge through our own, then show us how to transform them into love.

Their insights give us the strength and inspiration to find serenity amid the challenges of life. Most important, we feel compassionate for those we thought we could never love. Because of their search for love from their own mothers, they share with us the greatest love of all—their love for themselves.

Does the act of reading these letters and writing one of your own nurture feelings of love, even if it only begins as a tiny spot? Allow this spot to grow, and eventually you will experience the greatest love of all—the love of yourself.

The Butterfly on My Shoulder

As my children got older and they bickered with each other or defied my requests, I began to understand how a mother's emotions sporadically sway from anger to happiness to disappointment to warmth to fear to joy.
CAROLYN JOHNSON, *California*

Dear Mother,
Today I received a postal package from you for my sixty-first birthday and opened it to find a little book of poems and sayings from mothers to their daughters. I must admit my surprise because I don't think of you as being particularly sentimental. You don't save cards or photos, you don't like to see people cry, and friends love your quick sense of humor. Now it appears you've sent me an expanded, gushy birthday card.

Sitting in my chair with my paralyzed legs tied together, I began to peruse the book, expecting it to be a trite expression of caring. Instead, I was touched by notes you sprinkled throughout the pages, relating certain poems or sayings to our personal relationship. It was not a superficial gesture at all, but a very precious one.

One noted quote was by Debbie Reynolds: *The chasm that existed between us is now, thankfully, a meadowland of conversation and love.* I tipped my head back and let memories of our stormy past percolate through my mind. In these waning years of both our lives, how had we found our own meadow of beauty?

As a child, I adored you. You baked pies, put ironed white sheets on my bed, and curled my hair. You always sewed a pretty outfit for the first day of school, and once you let me help pluck feathers off the Thanksgiving turkey.

I remember us sitting close together as you carefully glued shiny sequins onto the full net skirt of a royal blue taffeta formal. I pictured you as the most beautiful mother at the dance. Once, you threw yourself across me to prevent my stepfather from hitting me. I wanted you to be perfect and you were.

As a young teenager, I became afraid of my perfect mother. Oh yes, you still ironed the sheets, still invited single neighbors who had no families to join our Thanksgiving dinner, and still hung the towels and pajamas in neat rows on the clothesline. But now you scolded or hit me if I was slow with my chores, or if I spoke in a sassy manner. Now you tried to push me into a prestigious social group and I balked.

"Why can't you be more like Linda Martin?" you would sometimes ask. The question haunted me for many years.

After you were hospitalized with a nervous breakdown, I feared that you would never come home again. When you did, you were often angry or unhappy. I wanted to be perfect for you, but I didn't know how to help. In another quote you had marked in the little book, Gail Godwin observes, *You never will finish being a daughter.*

In my older teenaged years, you reconnected with former friends and regained your health and sense of humor. I felt that you wanted us to be chums, but you also lectured and disciplined me.

When my friends joined us at the beach or at home or a boy came to dinner, you did most of the talking. You were clever and funny, while I felt boring. You cooked and I set the table. You had the talent and I was a drudge. You were pretty and lithe and I had pimples and gangly arms. Were you trying to compensate for my lack of spirit or competing for the attention of my peers?

It seemed you flirted with every man we knew, even my boyfriends and the butcher. Immodest behavior with my stepfather particularly irritated me, just at this time when I was wondering about becoming sexually active with boys. I shied away from talking to you about sex and chose to lie instead.

While you had come out of your lonely shell into a world of fun, I felt immersed in fear and confusion. More and more, conflict grew between us. We were ready to separate. In the book, you marked a quote by Erica Jong: *Letting go, I love you. Letting go, I hold you in my arms.*

After college, I married and began learning to become a parent while you tended to pull away from motherhood. You traveled the world, wore St. John knits, and played golf with Republicans. I lived in a world of Jefferson Airplane, Cost Plus, a government job, diapers, and Democrats. You bragged about how much you paid for an item and I bragged about how little I paid.

As my children got older and they bickered with each other or defied my requests, I began to understand how a mother's emotions sporadically sway from anger to happiness to disappointment to warmth to fear to joy. Yet all the while, I felt an underpinning of love and compassion for my children that was deeper than I'd ever encountered. As the mystery of motherhood enveloped me, I made comparisons to those times of stress between you and me.

Yes, we spent holidays together with backyard barbecues or dressy dinners, decorated trees, and piles of presents. Between times of laughter, we argued heatedly. I screamed at you for denigrating my husband, while you accused me of flirting with yours. We managed to hurt each other while not wanting to. Later, we learned that we were both in crummy marriages with degrees of abuse, but because we lived on a superficial plane, we didn't know we needed to help each other anymore.

As it happened, in the same year your husband died, I got a divorce. Five years later, we both married gentle, trustworthy men, and as time passed, we discovered there was no need to lie to each other anymore.

About three years ago, my husband was diagnosed with a rare disease, dermatomyositis. You called often, said prayers, and sent small gifts and cards to encourage us. My favorite gift was a tiny butterfly pin made of lavender crystal. I wore it every day, like having my mother sit on my shoulder.

Then came my own diagnosis two years ago of Lou Gehrig's disease (ALS). No drugs nor surgery nor implants nor therapy will arrest this illness. It is freewheeling and uncontrollable. It destroys muscles in a willy-nilly manner. Our whole family was devastated, but once again, you, Mother, showed your strength. You and dear Ed call daily, visit often, and send surprises and cards.

In the book, you marked this quote by Pam Brown: *Thank you for showing me, when I thought my mothering days were over, that the best days between us are only just beginning.* Mother, you have recaptured your rightful place as nurturer and wise guide. Between us, I feel no judgments, no lies, no competition, no struggle to become separate entities. We are simply friends, but also we are again mother and daughter. I welcome your cheerful nature and frequent compliments. I feel as content with you now as I did when, at ten years old, I'd come home from school and see you ironing sheets while country-western music blared on the radio.

In these tough years of my unpredictable health condition, I am blessed to have a living, vibrant, and very funny mother when I need you most. You are a constant, spirited, loving comfort, an anchor in a rough sea, a beautiful butterfly upon my shoulder. You are my guardian angel. Thank you, Mother. I wanted you to be perfect, and you are.

Love forever, no matter where we are, Carolyn

I've Never Felt Your Love

I might have had your love and didn't know it. I might have taken several small events and turned them into significant wounds.

MARIANNE SWIM, *Texas*

Dear Mom,

I've spent the past fifty years of my life thinking—*knowing*—that you didn't love me. All of my life's behaviors have sprung from this central piece of knowledge. This wounded child I carry around forms my overriding memories and is incorporated into every cell in my body.

Yesterday, my entire being was rocked to the core. I almost dismissed the thought that crossed my mind—that you did love me—but the insight hit me so hard, I had to sit down. I couldn't easily dismiss this new thought. Was it possible my life's truth was nothing more than a tightly wrapped package of illusion that I once experienced and which I refused to let go of?

We were a good example of a dysfunctional family. Dad

was an abusive drunk, but you held on to that proud southern tradition of staying married and carrying on appearances no matter what. Outwardly, we presented ourselves as a happy family. You choose to remember meaningful holidays, family meals, and good times. I only remember being scared all the time. Scared of being yelled at. Scared of getting beaten. Scared of doing something wrong that would set off an "episode."

Still, I was always the "good" kid—the middle one between the rebellious older daughter and beloved wayward son. My sister and brother hated our father for his drunken abusiveness, but I hated you for not doing anything about it. While the other two kids were showered with attention drawn by defiantly poor choices, I got good grades in school and never gave you grief. The few times I called for attention by getting into major trouble, you simply grounded me for a week and dismissed it as a fluke. But, alas, I was too shy and too scared to do much.

Somewhere along the way, I lost the hatred and just felt sorry for myself. My father loved liquor too much to love his children, and you simply loved the other two instead of me. So there I was, the good kid who, in reality, was a scared, shy kid filled with longing that my "real" parents would soon come and claim me. I would seek solace in my only friend, an imaginary horse that could take me to better places.

Before the end of high school, my sister ran away. Today she's in constant trouble with life—unsettled, divorced, and unhappy. My brother dropped out of school far too young and turned to liquor and drugs. He often runs afoul of the law. I left home to simply *be* somebody. Through it all, Mom, you kept up appearances.

You wanted marriage and kids for me, but I was too broken dealing with the child still inside me to handle a real-life child. I never had kids because I was never ready for them. I don't regret that decision. I was always afraid that I would transfer my emotional burden and scars onto my child, and I felt too sorry for myself to do that to someone else. So that's how it went for years. Fifty, to be exact.

And then, the seemingly insignificant event that changed how I view my life. The dog squabble—one of countless squabbles between Codo, the dominant dog, and Cali, the devilish fun-loving troublemaker. Codo is the calm dog that listens to commands, yet I spend all my time desperately teaching Cali to behave. Not to chase the cats. Not to chase the horses. Not to get on the furniture. I take her on walks to wear her out so she will not pester me with her toys and antics. I didn't have to spend a lot of time with the other dog, Codo, because she always did the right thing.

One day, I smacked Codo as Cali ran off. That's when it hit me. I was being unfair. My actions did not accurately reflect my feelings. Did Codo feel unloved or unwanted because I spent most of my time with Cali?

My allocation of time and attention did not equal my allocation of love for the dogs. I *loved* Codo. When I talked to friends about the dogs, I always praised Codo and complained about Cali. Yet I know that I spend most of my time with Cali and not with Codo.

Was I like a "Codo" for you, Mom? Did you love me too all this time? All these years of feeling lonely and feeling sorry for myself—I'll never know if it was a waste or not. But love? I might have had your love and didn't know it. I might have taken several small events and turned them into significant wounds.

The natural state of a horse is wandering in open land. Yet a racehorse that's been confined in a stall all his life and is suddenly let loose will run for all he's worth back to the confinement of his stall. It's what he's knows. Similarly, the process of replacing what I know with something new is challenging. A Jungian psychologist once said, "You have to give up the life you have in order to get the life that's waiting for you."

The memories are embedded in every cell of my brain and body, and nothing can change that. Like the racehorse, my changes will take time. Forgiveness has nothing to do with *you* and everything to do with *me*. The worst part is that I will never really know the truth. You say you loved me, but I didn't feel loved as a child. However, I can choose to let go of that wounded child, take this new insight, and wrap it up in a new, more positive reality. Over time, I can change my very being and thus change my future.

P.S. I hug Codo a lot these days. I give Codo special treats when Cali is outside finding trouble. I don't just *feel* it; I *show* Codo I love her. It's good for Codo, but it's better for me. It's my way of healing myself.

Truly, Marianne Swim

The Dreams We Had for Each Other

I still remember the day I was putting up screens in my kitchen and you said, "Now, honey, if you just had a husband, he could do that for you." I remember feeling annoyed as I reminded you, "I put up the screens all during my married life."

PATRICIA PAPE, *Illinois*

Dear Mom,

"It's a girl!" I never knew what these words conjured up for you. I never thought to ask. I know you had been waiting for thirteen years to have a child, had visited an adoption agency, and now you had me. I know that when *I* heard those words several years later, I was so excited. My son was two and I would have my daughter. What more could I ask?

I remember some of the struggles I had growing up in the '40s and '50s because you and I were different. I was more like my father and I suspect that was difficult for you. I also know that you lived a lot of your life vicariously through me. Your mother had died when you were eleven, and you got married very young, the month after you graduated from high school. You began your dreams for me: to be popular, to be a cheerleader, to be prom queen. I tried my best to please you and did well. I still remember the night I was crowned prom queen. You were in the front row of the balcony in the high school gymnasium and nearly fell over when they announced my name. I remember saying to my best friend, "They really should have given the crown to my mother because she worked much harder and wanted it much more than I did!"

I knew I had to go to college. But I also knew I had to get married. I married the boy you wanted me to, rather than the one I met my senior year and brought home to meet you and Dad. You said the boy you chose would be "more successful and provide for me better." And I took your advice. I have often wondered, now that we are divorced, what would have happened if I had followed my own instincts.

You became a victim of the medical system in the '70s, a system that labeled menopause a serious mental disease, and you were so medicated and depressed that I hardly knew you! Then when Dad died in the early '70s, you had become so dependent and helpless that you couldn't—didn't even want to—take care of yourself. I remember being so angry with you for that. By then, I was raising my two children as a single parent and working full-time. I tried having you live with me; I was going to "make you independent." But that failed and you went back to your assisted, medicated living. I felt terrible.

In the late '70s, I completed my master's of social work degree and launched my midlife career. Every time we'd get together, you would carefully point out all of the reasons I should be getting married rather than starting a career. I still remember the day I was putting up screens in my kitchen and you said, "Now, honey, if you just had a husband, he could do that for you." I remember feeling annoyed as I reminded you, "I put up the screens all during my married life."

One of my most poignant memories was Halloween night of 1981. My son, daughter, and I had spent weeks renovating the old house that would become the space for my own private group practice. My son built the big sign in the front yard: *PAPE & ASSOC.* In my office, I hung the special artwork you had given me of a country scene, painted by a friend of yours. I picked you up at the nursing home to show you this place that was my pride and joy. I later realized you had no idea of the significance of this event for me—even when you looked into my eyes, with love and sadness, and said, "Oh, honey, it's just too bad that you couldn't find a good man!" Those were your last words to me. You died five days later. Your dream for me never came true.

My daughter, now grown, is also a licensed clinical social

worker. I, too, had a dream for her. My dream was she would branch out, get some independent experience, then return to Chicago, eventually taking over the business that I'd started twenty years ago. She did the first half: went to California, got a job, met a man, got married, had two beautiful boys. I realize now she's never returning to Chicago.

So we are two mothers, each of whom had a dream for her daughter and neither of our dreams came true. I am learning only now, as a mother of a daughter, just how hard it is to let go—and to encourage our loved ones to fulfill their own dreams, to trust their own instincts, and to soar.

I love you,

Your daughter Patricia

Living Up to Your Expectations

If I could speak freely without fearing your rejection, I would be able to tell you what I need from our relationship.
AUDREY LITTLE, *Canada*

Dear Mom,

How can a person be honest with someone she's afraid to hurt?

This question has haunted me for the past few years, knowing that I need to set boundaries yet having no idea how to approach other members of the family. As a person who had perfected the art of taking things personally, I wouldn't expect anyone to listen with a nonjudgmental approach to issues surrounding a relationship. It's not an easy process for me and I know that it will not be easy for you either, but I hope you can listen to the thoughts as if they were coming from a friend.

As a child I often heard "I love you" but didn't consciously recognize the unconditional expectations attached to that love. Instinctively, I tried to become the perfect child, never letting you down. This meant working hard in school, participating in activities, and pursuing jobs you felt were worthy. If you were proud of me, then you would have to love me. Yet I never felt that I earned your love; in some way, I must be unlovable because I was different from my sister and my parents.

Sadly, this never really changed. It has been a constant struggle to be an independent adult who has your unconditional love. I have been unable to be honest about who I am for fear of you withdrawing your love. The result has been intolerable guilt and anger over not allowing myself to live my life for *me*.

This letter is my tool for unleashing the pent-up emotions that I've been feeling throughout my life. It's not intended to be hurtful to you. I have always felt an incredible bond between us and have enjoyed our time together. Lately, I have begun to feel that bond weaken to the point of being completely unsure of our relationship.

What I once thought was unconditional love is now clearly conditional. This may seem harsh; I know that you love me no matter what. However, this is not the message you have been providing throughout my life.

You have always had expectations of how I should act, what I should do, and what I should be. The result was growing up with a constant need to gain your love and approval.

Even after I'd left home, you continued to "control" the

person I would become. It isn't reasonable for a daughter to live her life for anyone, regardless of the love for and bond she feels with that person. In fact, much of the emotional pain I now try to expel has built as a result of this incredible pressure that I've felt. I'm an extremely sensitive individual and I'm aware that this scares you. I'm not sensitive just to make you uncomfortable; it's about being true to myself.

I don't believe that you consciously manipulated me, and so I have tried to tell you when I feel that my rights are being impinged upon. Understandably, you feel that I am attacking you. However, if you listen to the words that I'm saying, you will find that there is no attack intended.

If I could speak freely without fearing your rejection, I would be able to tell you what I need from our relationship. There are ten main points that need to be considered; each has the potential of creating a better relationship and, in some cases, building a stronger foundation that can withstand the passage of time.

Treat me as an adult and not as your child. I need the ability to live my life as an adult, not a child fearing retaliation from a disappointed mother. I am not the same person that you needed to protect as a small child. I am an intelligent and capable woman with experiences and knowledge to guide myself through the world.

Offer guidance and advice when I request it. (Nobody

likes to receive advice and guidance when they haven't asked for it.) Trust that I will ask you for your assistance when I need it. Allowing me to make my own decisions is allowing me to be who I am. In the same manner, I will return the favor and only offer suggestions and guidance when you seek it.

Remove expectations from our relationship. Love cannot be conditional; this means that you cannot expect me to live according to your expectations or rules of life. Approval or disapproval of me is neither part of the equation nor should it ever be.

Realize that I am a person in my own right who owes no explanations for how I live my life or what I do. Just as you expect things in your life to remain private or shared only with those you choose to share with, I expect the same considerations. I am an intelligent individual who needs to be able to live her life without interference. I am willing to take the results of any actions I initiate, whether the outcome is positive or negative.

I am not obligated to tell you anything about my financial, career, or personal life unless I choose to share it with you. Part of being a responsible adult is being able to choose what information you share with others and what information is relevant only to you. This doesn't mean that I won't share information; it just means that I will let you know when I have things to share.

Provide notice of when you think you would like to come to visit. If you receive unexpected guests, you feel unhappy, taken advantage of, and sometimes even downright angry. These feelings are completely normal. Please realize that I may have the same feelings regarding unannounced visits, leading to anger and frustration on my part.

Understand that it is not a familial obligation for you to stay in my home. It is nice to have a place to stay when you travel. However, it does not guarantee that I will be open to having company.

Understand that sometimes I am not available for conversations or visits. In the same way that you dislike being put on the spot, so do I.

Remove the competition between us. Our childhoods were not the same, nor were our experiences after we left home. If I share frustrations with you, I am not looking to hear that your childhood was worse than mine. I am sharing with you a story and not looking to compete with you over past experiences.

Allow me to be who I am and love me for the strength of my courage, convictions, and desire to live a full and happy life, which may mean doing things that you might disapprove of. It is not your role to approve or disapprove of how I live my life.

Following these ten steps will provide an enriched relationship, built on the understanding that love is not conditional upon pleasing one another. Our relationship can grow, evolve, and strengthen when we both begin to see the boundaries that need to exist for a healthy relationship. Until then, there will be continued feelings of resentment over the expectations that you have placed upon provision of your love.

I do not believe for one moment that you do these things intentionally; in fact, I think that it is most likely you have no idea that you are overstepping any boundaries. It is for this reason that I write this letter. Maybe recognition of individual differences will make things easier for both of us.

It is because I value our relationship and the bond that we share that I have been willing to share my feelings with you. You will never read this letter, which made it so much easier to write. It is a healing experience to finally let go of some things that haunted me until just recently.

I clearly can admit I love you and know that you love me in the way that you best know how.

Love, your daughter

Saving Grace

Unloved, you had no idea how to give love. Your willingness to forgive your mother, even as you still carried the scars, astonished me, and I realized that now, in the closing years of your life, I could do no less.

CAROLYN PIPER, *Vermont*

Dear Mom,

I remember well that spring morning you hurled your wallet at me and screamed, "I told you not to come!" A month earlier, you had been diagnosed with Alzheimer's. The soup I made for you went flying one way, the tray another, and from way deep down came one last cry of "Mom!" Our role reversal, well under way, came full circle.

Watching the soup dribble down the wall, I saw terror etched in your eyes. "God help me. God help me. Please don't let me last long!" you cried, wrapping your arms around yourself and rocking back and forth. I was horrified, yet wonder filled me as I realized for the first time that I was hearing simple emotional truth from a woman who had always been an enigma to me.

You never liked to face reality. You fought for so long to make life and those around you as you wanted them to be. In the process, you strained our relationship to the breaking point. There was fault on both sides. You were always socially conscious, concerned with niceties and appearance, while I—bookish and rebellious—was hard of hearing as a result of a childhood illness. This made me socially inept and, briefly, a scholastic failure in a family of achievers.

I was frightened of you. Your glare when you felt a social rule had been transgressed could freeze me.

When Dad died and you decided to move to a retirement village in my city, I screamed. I cried. I described in detail the horrible cold winters we have. I pointed out how far you would be from friends and finally became downright nasty in hopes of scaring you off.

Of course you came anyway. And a year later, I was staring at a soup-stained wall and facing the fact that, panicked beyond your ability to cope, like it or not, I was in the driver's seat.

Psychotic episodes followed increasing memory loss. Medical decisions had to be made. Financial decisions. Emotional decisions. The first two were easy, the last more problematic. Here you were at my mercy and the choices were mine: I could advocate for you financially and medically while ignoring the person within, or I could, for heaven's sake, rob you blind. What I could *not* do was care deeply.

I became an advocate for your care, keeping a wary eye out lest I be emotionally blindsided again. Instead, I found the saving grace of a gradual terminal illness. Antidepressants and antianxiety medication made a terrific, and positive, difference for you. So, amazingly, did the Alzheimer's itself. As your memory faded, so too did the defenses you had built. And for the first time in our lives, we talked. Sitting in your room, safe among your cherished possessions, you shared your past with me.

"Do you know," you asked me one day as we sat together, "what it's like to grow up feeling hated?"

"Tell me, Mom," I answered. Then you told me the story of a little girl who had never felt loved a day in her life—who finally learned the reason when she went sleigh riding on a sled when she was ten years old. You told me, "After one run, I turned to see a friend and she yelled at me: 'Your mom isn't your mom.' All I could do was run home to see Mama."

Your mother (Mom-Mom as we grandchildren called her) was baking cookies when you burst in the door and asked *the* question. Turning to you, the woman you had always called Mother calmly told you it was nothing to concern yourself about. "Your father's first wife died when you were born," she said as if she were talking about a change in the dinner menu rather than an emotional avalanche. "He and I got married when you were two. It wasn't a matter of loving you," she went on as she put another batch of cookies in the oven. "You came with your father and I had no choice but to take you on."

I spent a life longing for a mother. And my children missed the legacy of love from a grandmother who was smart and caring, with a crackerjack sense of humor. We all paid for that absence of love, for in its absence, people wilt and die. We erect defenses around ourselves to protect ourselves from the hurt we've come to see as inevitable.

Your willingness to forgive such a thing, even as you still carried the scars, astonished me. I realized that now, in the closing years of your life, I could do no less. I realized the truth of the words of W.H. Auden that we must "love one another or die."

Love, Carolyn

The Need for Closure: A Loving Word from Lisa

Writing this letter to my mother became an important catalyst in my personal healing process. It helped me see more clearly how I had come thus far, and what would be the next steps I would take. As a psychologist, I believe in the utility of journaling and letter writing. As a daughter, I know about its power.

MARISOL MUÑOZ KIEHNE, PH.D., *California*

At dinner, a man I'd just met asked me if I thought writing a letter could create more peace in the world. After thinking about the extraordinary results of this Project, I responded, "Writing just one letter to your mother will guide you to open your heart fully, release pent-up emotion, and produce a transformation in yourself, therefore in the world. The more we are committed to work through our fears, the more insightful and peaceful we will become. For every time your own heart lightens up, there is a positive effect in the world and you can see the light in others."

At the time my mother almost died, all I knew was how fearful I felt about her leaving. My intention in writing my letters to my mother was to release the pain within me and let her know how grateful I was for her. I listened to myself and trusted the process, knowing eventually I would be in a better place. Just as I needed to express my feelings to my mother, she deeply needed to hear what I said in the letters. Amazingly, that one step toward closure created a new opening in both our hearts and, as we healed, began a new chapter in both our lives.

My mother wrote, "One sad day, I almost passed away. Lisa wrote letters from the heart asking for me to stay. In her letters to Mom at this time, she wrote (and I shall quote): 'I love you with every fiber of my being.' One of the reasons God brought me back was to put Lisa on the right track."

To this day, my mother keeps the letters I wrote to her displayed beautifully in a book cover on her table. She frequently reads them as if for the first time. "This is something one reads in an obituary. I am fortunate to have received this precious gift while I'm alive and well," she says.

As Barbara Hinkle says, "I found that writing the letter to my mother served as a catharsis for me. Mother had been dead twenty-three years when I wrote the letter, and I had been in recovery for three years. I had begun to know myself for the first time, and in so learning, I had explored my feelings about my alcoholic mother. I had thought that I hated her, and I blamed her for hurting me with her alcoholism. I have come to realize that my mother was truly ill and was unable to stop drinking, though she tried several times. I now have frequent 'conversations' with her and feel in my heart that she is hearing me and helping me maintain the strength she was not able to garner."

What truly gives us the most freedom in our lives is the willingness to work through our wounds instead of dwelling on them, to prevail victorious beyond our circumstances, and to employ all of our challenges to better ourselves. Resolution gives us the chance to truly begin anew, reconnecting to our joyous hearts once again.

Fordena Griffith says, "I used to think resolution meant having every stray word accounted for, both words spoken and heard. But sometimes willingness to make peace with the past must be enough. The letter-writing process—for me and for my relationship with my mom—was a beginning. And every great journey must have one of those."

A Loving Word from Lisa

I hope you take these women's insights as a guide to explore your own relationship with your mother and, most important, with yourself. I encourage you to nurture your emotions, heal your wounds, and always unearth the possibilities of growth that lie within you.

I wish for every daughter who has or has had a great relationship with her mother to continue to treasure all those precious moments. If you're struggling with your mother or any other challenge in your life, my greatest prayer is that you're able to courageously do the work necessary to free yourself and find the light you are searching for. You deserve this chance.

May you make it a priority to tend to unresolved matters and discover the purpose of compassion, peace, and love throughout your life.

An Invitation to You

Writing this letter can take more courage than anything you have ever done. I came away understanding how I perceived the relationship with my mother and how it had impacted my life. I encourage others to partake in this letter-writing process. The experience is truly amazing and more empowering than you would dare to dream.

AUDREY LITTLE, *Canada*

The Letters from the Heart Project™ offers much insight and assistance in releasing emotional barriers and finding liberation within. As you work through uncovering your emotions, we are here to support, listen, and guide you through the process. We invite you to participate in our upcoming Heartshops™, teleclasses, and other educational programs. To learn about these opportunities and how to participate in the Share-A-Heart Foundation™, please visit our Web site at www.LettersFromTheHeartProject.com.

Many have asked to read the letters that I wrote to my mother. I did not include them in this book. However, they are posted on my Web site, www.LisaDelman.com. I felt it most important to honor my commitment to the women whose letters were selected for this book and capture the emotions and core issues of the heart through their varied experiences. Also posted on my Web site are the women's responses to my questions about how the letter-writing process affected them and their relationships with their mothers. Their results are awe inspiring. A resource list is available on the Web site to further support women dealing with the issues mentioned in this book: breast cancer, Alzheimer's, sexual abuse, mental illness, alcoholism, death and dying, drug addiction, sexuality, teenage homelessness, adoption, and so on.

To send correspondence via the postal service, please write to: Lisa R. Delman, Letters from the Heart Project, 12555 Biscayne Blvd, # 775, North Miami, FL 33181-2597.

Ten Ways to Open Your Heart to Your Mother

1. Honor Yourself

Take a few moments to honor and appreciate yourself. Acknowledge your courage to open your heart, articulate your emotions on paper, and grow from your willingness to write the letter to your mother. When you take the time to reflect inwardly, you nurture yourself.

2. Reconnect to Your Heart

Take some deep breaths and connect emotionally with your mother. Self-reflection requires a change of pace from what we are accustomed to. Allow yourself the time to relax. Perhaps choose a favorite place in nature, listen to soothing music such as Enya, Steve Halpern, or classical music, or enjoy your favorite food or tea. Create a quiet, private space to write your letter.

3. Create a Desired Outcome

Creating an intention for the result of your letter guides you to be more focused on what is important. Expand your thoughts beyond your present image of your mother and your relationship. For example, you may want to resolve past hurts, be more loving toward her, or work your way toward forgiveness. The key is to concentrate on resolution.

4. Express Feelings Honestly

Choose one or two of the emotions listed below that make you think of your mother and write about them. This exercise is about acknowledging a specific feeling, releasing it, and learning from it in a meaningful way. To release a negative feeling, you might want to write about that feeling and see what you discover about yourself in the process. If it is a positive feeling, you may discover something new about your mother. Remember, this is a springboard to guide you. Only you know what is true in your heart.

- Fear
- Embarrassment
- Joy, Celebration, Enthusiasm
- Sorrow, Sadness, Regret, Remorse, Grief, Guilt
- Freedom, Letting Go, Joy, Release
- Gratitude, Appreciation, Respect

• Courage, Bravery, Risk Taking
• Control, Regret, Bossiness, Criticism
• Epiphany, Forgiveness, Insight
• Resentment, Anger, Betrayal, Jealousy, Competition, Estrangement
• Love, Understanding, Acceptance, Compassion, Forgiveness, Peace of Mind

5. Appreciate All of the Memories

Be grateful for all of the memories you have with your mother and learn from them. Recall defining moments, challenging times, or particular gestures. You may not know how you feel until you put pen to paper. Simply let your ideas unfold naturally without forcing them. Welcome your uncensored emotions without judgments. If judgments arise, gently release them as part of the process. Be patient and loving to yourself.

6. Explore Different Perspectives

We view our relationships according to our perspective on life. Many times, we cannot see beyond our own experiences. As you think of your relationship with your mother, begin viewing her in various roles in her life: as a woman, wife, daughter, grandmother, volunteer, professional, and friend. Seeing your mother in a new light can provide a fresh perspective on the way you view her, yourself, and your relationship.

Write down five or more things you've noticed about yourself and your mother when you explore these different roles.

7. Think From Generation to Generation

As daughters, we primarily focus on the relationship with only our mothers. We blame our mothers for the beliefs they may have adopted from their mothers, and so on. If we explore the past, we notice that certain behaviors have been passed on to us from generation to generation.

Jot down five of these belief systems. If you are not sure about those in other generations, speculate and write them down anyway.

8. Go Beyond Stereotypical Expectations

We often expect our mothers to be a certain way from the cultural messages we grew up with, and when they do not meet our image, we feel disappointed and even resentful. Often, our expectations cloud us from appreciating our mothers for who they are. Once we can identify with our false expectations, we can honor their uniqueness.

Jot down five expectations you have now or once had with your mother. Also write down what you discovered from this process.

9. Make Challenges Your Greatest Gifts

We often blame our mothers for the all the hardships we experienced while growing up and the hardships we still experience: for not being there, for being there in the "wrong way", for the women we are, for the women we are not, for all the challenges we had to overcome because of our mothers. Many times, our challenges turn into resentments, which prevent us from being in the present moment.

Write down five resentments you have about your mother. Explore your challenges with your mother as gifts and write down what you discover.

10. Open Your Heart

The objective of these ten exercises is to examine your relationship with your mother from new perspectives and open your heart. When we view our experiences in new ways, we enrich our relations with others and ourselves. Feel free to use some or all of these exercises to support you in writing your letter.

Congratulations. You have already begun writing your letter. Be true to your personal voice; it will always lead you to the right place. The rest will follow.

About the Author

Lisa R. Delman is founder and facilitator of the international Letters from the Heart Project™, which was born out of her cathartic experience after her mother suffered a near-fatal heart attack. She encourages women to articulate their emotions on paper via letter writing—initiating a journey that often leads to self-discovery, and healing past wounds. Lisa now works passionately connecting hearts of the world, through her speaking engagements, Heartshops™, tele-classes, and upcoming relationship book series.

Lisa has a master's of arts degree in organizational design and effectiveness, and utilizes her communication and marketing skills to create goodwill in all her endeavors. She lives with her husband, John, and their two dogs and two cats in Miami, Florida.